SPARKLES OF MAGIC

Amethyst Healing Properties

First edition

This book was professionally typeset on Reedsy.
Find out more at reedsy.com

Contents

I

Part One

One

My Crystal Healing Journey

My crystal healing journey and my love for crystals started about year 2009.

My only sanctuary and peace I had was visiting the library daily i would go there at 5pm and come home after 10pm at closing times. One day, as I browsed through the new age books, I noticed a crystal healing book and thought I would borrow this. When I got home, and read about Rose Quartz and its healing properties, I was well surprised Rose Quartz heals trauma and abuse, and even showers you with the love energy. I thought no doctor on earth could heal me with this, but these crystals can. So the next day I went back to the library to use the computer where i looked up crystal healing stores near me, which i visited the next time I got paid. When I visited the Crystal Store, I was like a child in a toy shop. The crystals appeared so pretty. I ended up buying five of them for £5.00. There was Rose Quartz, Smoky Quartz, Amethyst and another one and i had no idea how to use them, so I placed them anywhere on my body. By 2020, I have done tons of crystal healing, and I know where to place them. Thanks to Judy Hall crystal prescription books. I have healed many issues and feel so much better. I have gained so much knowledge in crystal healing by reading books and Google Search, and I have completed a crystal healing and advanced crystal healing diploma.

Two

Amethyst Physical Healing

Amethyst boosts the production of hormones and stimulates the sympathetic nervous system and endocrine glands to optimum performance. It supports oxygenation in the blood, and aids in treatments of the digestive tract, heart, stomach, and skin. Amethyst also strengthens the immune system and reduces bruising, pain and swellings. It has been used with excellent results as an elixir in the treatment of arthritis.

Amethyst is supposed to relieve the symptoms of tinnitus and other hearing disorders, and is highly beneficial in treating insomnia, especially when caused by an overactive mind. It is calming and soothing to the neural impulses in the brain. Its energy ameliorates the pain of headaches and migraines, and reduces stress and nervous tension. It may be used to treat psychic disturbances and stabilize brain imbalances. Amethyst boosts production of hormones and tunes the endocrine system and metabolism. It strengthens the cleansing and eliminating of organs, as well as the immune system, and is an excellent blood cleanser. Amethyst relieves physical, emotional and psychological pain or stress.

It's an excellent healing crystal for people who have or are recovering from cancer. It's a wonderful combination of healing and calming.

It is also known as the sobering stone, suitable for all forms of addiction, from alcoholism to anorexia. If you suffer with either of these, or love someone who does, a good sized piece of Amethyst under their bed will work while they sleep (though it also has a sobering effect on the libido, so bear that in mind! :)).

Along those lines, it is also said to be a wonderful antidote for a hangover or headache. Take a smooth stone and rub gently on your temples for a few minutes to dissolve the head clouds. **Amethyst is an excellent crystal to enhance physical vitality, especially after chemotherapy, radiation, or pharmaceutical treatments.**

It's an energizing healer on a physical level. Because it can strengthen the adrenal glands, the reproductive organs, and the heart.

It can help treat disorders that affect the lungs, pancreas, and spleen. It can also stimulate fertility and help treat conditions related to the reproductive system.

Amethyst can strengthen the immune system. It can also help you achieve a speedy recovery from a severe illness.

It can be effective in cell regeneration. Natural amethyst is well-known as a stress reliever and can also detoxify the body.

Three

Cleansing Your Amethyst

Before you buy your healing crystals, you have to learn how to heal them and look after them.

Always make sure your crystals are cleansed. Cleansing means removing all unhealthy and negative energies, your own, and other people's negative and harmful energies from them. Do this before and after working with them, to do this work with a natural method of cleaning your negative energies from the crystals.

I found out what works best for me and my crystals, which took years to find. This is filling my sink with cold water, and putting one cup of Epsom salts in the bowl of water, and placing the healing crystals in the water, and leaving them in the water for one hour. You can also put your crystal under a running tap of cold water for a few seconds for a quick cleanse.

HOW TO STORE YOUR CRYSTALS

You can store your crystals in a natural box, like a wooden box, rattan box or wicker sea grass box, as natural products are grounding for your crystals.

And to store each individual crystal, you can store them in a natural jute hessian gift bag and have a natural kraft gift card label with the crystal's name on the card, or you could sew or embroidery with organic cotton the name of the crystal on the bag with the crystal's name on it. Looking after your crystals this way, they will be pleased crystal beings, have the most respect for them, love, and be grateful for all that they do for you.

Four

Amethyst And Meditation

Amethyst is one of the best crystals for meditation. The Amethyst color purple stimulates the highest vibration of the Third Eye, and placing an Amethyst stone directly over this area ushers in a serene meditative state that stills conscious thought and guides the mind toward deeper understanding. Its energy encourages the mind to be humble and surrender to that greater than itself, to gain some understanding of how the powers of the universe can direct and guide one's life.

To relax the system and increase awareness, hold single Amethyst crystals or small clusters in the left hand (termination towards the arm) during meditation to draw Amethyst energy into the body. Large clusters of Amethyst are ideal for meditation altars or concentration objects to train the mind to be centered and calm, while awareness is focused on the objective world.

Five

Amethyst Spiritual Healing

Amethyst stimulates the higher mind to receive one's spiritual power as a creation of the Divine being, and to open to the insights, wisdom, and guidance offered.

Amethyst is a stone of spiritual protection and purification; cleansing one's energy field of negative influences and attachments. It creates a resonant shield of spiritual light around the body. Additionally, it acts as a barrier against lower energies, psychic attack, geopathic stress, and unhealthy environments. It is a valuable protection for those doing psychic or intuitive work. And it's also an excellent psychic protection, especially during spiritual and physical travels.

Amethyst stimulates intuition and all psychic abilities, promoting a higher sense of consciousness. It's powerful for meditation and lucid dreams, supporting the connection between physical and spiritual. It is a wonderful all-purpose stone for working with psychic and mental energy, because it supports intuition, Divine connection, and higher states of consciousness, while simultaneously protecting you from negative energy as you open yourself up to receive information.

Six

Amethyst For The Aura

Amethyst high frequency purifies the aura of any negative energy or attachments, and creates a protective shield of light around the body.

Amethyst heals holes in the aura, cleanses it, draws in divine energy to protect the aura.

Amethyst helps transmute negative energies into positive ones. It also works for your aura, since everything is energy.

To heal your aura (subtle bodies), get an Amethyst and stroke downwards in the air around your body. Do the front, back and sides about seven to 50 times in each direction. You can lay down whilst you do this.

Another way to heal your aura (subtle bodies) is to put crystals on the floor in a grid, like a clock's face. Place a crystal at six o'clock and one at three o'clock, then lay down in the middle of the crystals with them around your body about a few inches from your body.

Healing your Chakras will heal your subtle bodies.

Your Subtle Energy Bodies

The Etheric Body

Everything that exists in the physical plane, like trauma and injuries that hold them memories in the Etheric body. The etheric body is linked to the Base chakra.

The emotional body
The emotional body is linked to the Sacral Chakra.

The Lower Mental Body

The lower mental body receives, stores and transmits all our thought patterns and mental processes. It is linked to the Solar Plexus.

The Higher Mental Body

The higher mental body is the layer of energy linked to the Heart Chakra.

The Causal Body

The Causal chakra is the doorway to higher consciousness and links personality to the collective consciousness of the planet.

The causal body is the layer of energy beyond the higher mental body, and is linked to the Throat Chakra and the causal chakra at the back of the head. Gifts and talents that you have attained in previous lives are sealed into your causal body and Throat chakra.

The Soul Body

This body holds the essence of your spirit – the part of you that is of God. Linked to the Brow chakra.

The Integrated Spiritual Body

Linked to the Crown Chakra.

Seven

The subtle bodies and different planes of existence

WHAT ARE THE SUBTLE BODIES?

Our energy points, energetic layers and subtle bodies create an interconnected field of energy around the physical body that is commonly known as the auric field. Each subtle body connects into the physical body via an energy point or chakra, which directs the energy into the physical body via the Meridian system.

Each subtle body corresponds to a subtle plane of existence that reach a point in the physical form. The different planes of existence have different worlds and universes, and each has a subtle body.

The Etheric Layer or first layer of your Aura

is associated with the physical aspects and awareness of your material body, and is related to the First (Root) Chakra.

As it is nearest to the human body, it is the densest, but is on the next higher vibrational level to the physical body, which has the lowest vibrational level.

It bridges the connection between your material or physical body to your higher bodies or subtle energy bodies.

The Etheric layer extending only about 10 millimeters (one-quarter inch) to 50 millimeters (two inches) beyond your physical body.

Your Emotional Layer or Second Layer of your Aura

is associated with your vibrational level of inner feelings and related to the Second (Sacral Plexus) Chakra, the emotional aspects of your life and being. This layer is extremely influential in both the higher and lower layers, and is crucial, as it influences your health profoundly.

The emotional layer or second layer of your aura is visible between 25 millimeters (one inch) to 75 millimeters (three inches) beyond your body.

The Mental layer or Third Layer of your Aura

Is associated with the vibrational level of thoughts and mental processes of your ego, and is related to the Third (Solar Plexus) Chakra, as well as your personal power. The mental layer contains the structure of your ideas reflecting your linear thinking processes, and your thought forms can also be seen in this layer.

The stronger and more ingrained these thought forms are, the greater their definition within your mental body.

The mental layer or the third layer of your aura also extends about 75 millimeters (three inches) to 20 centimeters (eight inches) from your physical body.

Your Astral layer or Fourth Layer of your Aura

Is associated with areas of expression on a physical, emotional and mental level, and is related to your Fourth (Heart) Chakra.

This layer is called the bridge between the denser or lower vibrations of the physical plane and the finer or higher vibrations of the spiritual planes.

In other words, it is not only the dividing line, but also connects the lower three layers with the higher three.

It is the layer within your Aura through which all energy must pass when going from one world to the other. It is the layer of love, both specific and universal, and the first of the spiritual layers. It is the doorway to the Astral plane.

The astral layer or the fourth layer of the aura extends between 30 centimeters (one foot) to approximately 45 centimeters (one and a half feet) beyond the physical body.

The Etheric Template or Fifth Layer of your Aura is associated with aspects of your physical body and is related to the Fifth (Throat) Chakra.

This layer holds the blueprint / template of all that exists on the physical plane.

The Etheric Template or the fifth layer of the aura is more structured and extends between 45 centimeters (one and a half feet) to about 60 centimeters (two feet) beyond your physical body.

The Celestial Layer or Sixth Layer of your Aura is associated with processes of enlightenment and related to your Sixth (Brow or Third Eye) Chakra.

And is also known as the intuitive level. This layer gives you access to higher qualities of feelings, thoughts and manifestations.

It is the level through which you experience spiritual ecstasy.

The celestial layer or the sixth layer of your Aura extends between 60 centimeters (two feet) to about 85 centimeters (two and three quarters feet) beyond your physical body.

The Ketheric Template or Seventh Level of your Aura is associated with the Divine or Universal Consciousness and is related to the Seventh (Crown) Chakra.

The seventh layer contains your *life plan or soul contract,* and reflects all experiences and events that your soul has ever experienced.

Also, containing all the auric bodies associated with the present incarnation you are undergoing.

The Ketheric Template or the seventh auric layer is the Mental Aspect on the Spiritual Level.

The Ketheric Template or the seventh layer of the Aura extends between 75 centimeters (two and a half feet) to about 90 centimeters (three feet) beyond your physical body.

In my research about the subtle bodies i found that one side is the conscious, and the other is the unconscious. Down below, below your feet is Hell, and up above, above your head is Heaven. So measure the subtle body points to the left, right, and down below and up above, and place an Amethyst at them points all around your body, so you will need to lay on the floor to heal.

The subtle bodies or your aura reflect your health, character, mental activity and emotional state.

It also shows dis-ease (on the higher plane) - often even long before it shows in the etheric layer and before the actual manifestation of symptoms in your physical body.

To heal each of your subtle bodies with your healing crystal, measure with a clothes tape measure at each point of each subtle body. The measurements are in each description of each subtle body, then place your Amethyst on them points.

II

Part Two

Eight

Amethyst Emotional Healing

Amethyst is especially supportive of the emotional body, bringing those who are overworked, over stressed, or overwhelmed back to center. It eases the mental anxieties that lead to physical tension and headaches, and is an excellent crystal to calm those who tend to be hot-headed and easily angered.

Amethyst helps identify the root causes behind one's negative behaviors, habits, and emotional patterns that create imbalance and disease. It also helps understand the reality of cause and effect in behavior, and helps in better decision-making. Emotionally, Amethyst is used in crystal healing to help heal personal losses and grief, bringing you gently past painful experiences.

It can also bring emotional stability and inner strength. It will get rid of grief, despair, anger, or defeat. It will soothe emotional wounds and alleviate the pain that comes with emotional trauma. Amethyst can help you confront your emotional issues and overcome them. It can bring your hidden or suppressed feelings to the surface so that something positive will take place. Amethyst energies can give you comfort when you need it. You will never feel alone. Because you will find a way to be happy and content even if you are alone. It works deeply on the emotional level to help build the skill to recognize emotional patterns. This crystal attracts positive energy and helps remove negative emotions, like fear, depression, and anxiety. Amethyst brings calmness and clarity, and is a wonderful stone when working in times of confusion or chaos. It promotes inner peace, and helps raise our vibrations. Amethyst has the awesome ability to transmute negative energy into love energy, leaving us feeling calm and serene. It can also transmute low vibrations into higher vibrations. Excellent stone for balancing uneven emotions and getting rid of harmful energy. **Amethyst can help transform impatience and anger into calmness and contentment.**

Nine

Amethyst And Wealth

Amethyst is an excellent crystal to have when you're serious about building your personal wealth. It will help grow your business, or share your abundance with the people you love.

Ten

Amethyst Healing Properties

Amethyst is a powerful and protective stone, and it creates a bubble around the carrier, warding off psychic attacks and negative energy. It guards against psychic attack, transmutes the energy into love, and protects the wearer from all types of harm, including geopathic or electromagnetic stress and ill wishes, assisting in transmuting negative energies within the wearer and protecting them from external negative energies. Amethyst is a natural tranquilizer, relieves stress and strain, soothes irritability, balances mood swings, dispels anger, rage, fear and anxiety. Alleviates sadness and grief, and dissolves negativity. This way it can promote calm, balance, and peace. Amethyst activates spiritual awareness, opens intuition and enhances psychic abilities. It has strong healing and cleansing powers. Amethyst encourages sobriety, having a sobering effect on overindulgence of alcohol, drugs or other addictions. It calms and stimulates the mind, helping you become more focused, enhancing memory and improving motivation. Amethyst helps remember and understand dreams. It relieves insomnia. Encourages selflessness and spiritual wisdom.

Amethyst boosts hormone production, tunes the endocrine system and metabolism. It strengthens the immune system, reduces pain, and strengthens the body to fight cancer. It destroys malignant tumors and aids in tissue regeneration. Cleanses the blood. Relieves physical, emotional and psychological pain or stress. Amethyst eases headaches and releases tension. It reduces bruising, swelling, injuries, and treats hearing disorders. Amethyst heals diseases of the lungs and respiratory tract, skin conditions, cellular disorders and diseases of the digestive tract. Amethyst was reputed to control evil thoughts, increase intelligence. Amethyst is still a remarkable stone of spirituality and contentment, known for its metaphysical abilities to still the mind and inspire an enhanced meditative state. Its inherent high frequency purifies the aura of any negative energy or attachments, and creates a protective shield of light around the body, allowing one to remain clear and centered while opening to spiritual direction. Amethyst stimulates the Third Eye, Crown, and Etheric Chakras, enhancing cognitive perception and accelerating the development of intuitive and psychic ability. It initiates wisdom and greater understanding, and is a stone of comfort for those grieving the loss of a loved one.

Amethyst's ability to expand the higher mind also enhances one's creativity and passion. It strengthens the imagination and intuition, and refines the thinking processes. It helps in the assimilation of new ideas, puts thought into action, and brings projects to fruition. Amethyst is also well-known as a talisman of focus and success. Amethyst protects against psychic attack, paranormal harm or ill-wishing, and returns the energy back to the universe after being transformed into positive, loving energy. Amethyst calms and soothes, assisting the transmission of neural signals through the brain. It relieves obsessive-compulsive disorder and hyperactivity in children and animals. Place under the pillow or mattress, or rub the center of the forehead counter-clockwise to cure insomnia and stimulate pleasant dreams. It is especially effective for children's recurring nightmares and fears of the dark, and may help alleviate homesickness.

Amethyst is an excellent stone for diplomats, negotiators, and business people. It calms angry temperaments and gives a distinct advantage in situations where debating is required. Wear or hold Amethyst to bring spiritual insights coupled with intellectual reasoning. As a luck and prosperity crystal, Amethyst is beneficial for reducing the tendency to overspend, gambling addictions or unwise investments. It is a stone dedicated to curbing overindulgence and bad habits, and is an excellent aid to quitting smoking, drinking, and drug use, as well as unhealthy physical passion. It also provides the strength needed to obtain freedom from addictive personalities, one's own or another. It is also known as the sobering stone, suitable for all forms of addiction, from alcoholism to anorexia. If you suffer with either of these, or love someone who does, a good sized piece of Amethyst under their bed, at the head end, will work while they sleep (though it also has a sobering effect on the libido, so bear that in mind! :)).

Along those lines, it is also said to be a wonderful antidote for a hangover or headache. Take a smooth stone and rub gently on your temples for a few minutes to dissolve the head clouds. It is also the perfect calming antidote for rage and anger. It also brings peace, insight and calmness, and helps insomnia sufferers sleep more easily. it is helpful in purifying the mind and clearing it of negative thoughts. **Amethysts can help you cut through tough situations and understand what you're dealing with.** They allow them to get through tough choices and decision-making processes as painlessly as possible. And if you are a natural empath or otherwise highly sensitive to your emotional environment, keep an amethyst stone by. It helps root you in reality and solid facts. **Amethyst can help manifest your true self, rather than be influenced by others to conform to other people's expectations.** Sometimes you feel uncomfortable with yourself. Amethyst can help you get rid of the shame and disappointment to get to the heart of the issue. It will also help you identify root causes or old hurts that lead to ways of behaving that you don't like about yourself. It can eliminate destructive actions and ideas, and replace them with only affirmative, empowering, and uplifting ones. Amethyst is recognized as a stone of spirituality and contentment. It enhances spiritual awareness and promotes a higher state of consciousness. Amethyst stimulates the third eye crown and etheric chakras. It helps enhance cognitive perception, as well as accelerate the development of intuitive and psychic abilities. It was reputed to control evil thoughts and increase intelligence. It initiates wisdom and greater understanding. It helps develop an ability to think more clearly and decision-making. It also helps in the assimilation of new ideas and putting thoughts into action. It has a positive effect on creativity and imaginative power by enhancing the intuition. Amethyst helps you break free from addictions, including food, sex, prescription and non-prescription drugs. Amethyst relieves physical, emotional and psychological pain or stress. Amethyst treats insomnia and brings restful sleep. Amethyst eases headaches, diseases of the brain and head, and improves motivation, making you more able to set realistic goals. Amethyst can stabilize psychiatric conditions, but should not be used in cases of paranoia or schizophrenia. It transmutes lower energies to the higher frequencies of the spiritual and etheric realms. This stone will help balance the left and right hemispheres of the brain. The amethyst also purifies negative energy and transmutes it into positive energy, which will improve the joy you experience in your life. It boosts our ability to love ourselves, which makes us more likely to pursue our passions and express our authenticity. This stone is wonderful for cleansing and removing negative energy within our body and space. It calms an overactive mind and blocks negative energies. By wearing the protective Amethyst crystal, one gets protection from all types of suffering, including spiritual assault, and those that may be due to external sources, including people. *Another great thing to work with Amethyst is to attempt to curb unhealthy habits, if it's wasting money, eating junk, the temptation to gamble, etc.*

Eleven

Amethyst For Love And Relationships

Deep and searching conversations with your partner can leave you both feeling a little vulnerable and uneasy. It's always best to keep an Amethyst close by for this reason. This crystal's energies will help you understand your own needs, wants, and desires in your relationship. Amethyst will stimulate your heart and open yourself up to more love. It will break down your walls, and it will release all your fears and worries about love. Amethyst can help remove the lethargy in your relationship. With hard work and commitment, you can restore what was lost. And it will also let you rekindle the passion missing. Amethyst can't help but stir up love and affection within you. **Amethyst is also known to promote better relationships on an intellectual, cerebral level.** It's known as a stone of comfort for those grieving the loss of a loved one.

How to Feng Shui Your Bedroom with an Amethyst

Crystal

1. Gather an amethyst cluster and a piece of red string.
2. From the view of lying on the bed, place the amethyst crystal underneath the bottom right-hand side of the bed.
3. Tie the red string around the amethyst and to the foot of the bed. The red string activates fidelity within the relationship and prevents other people from entering the relationship.
4. Traditionally, the husband, or masculine partner, should sleep on the left-hand side, and the woman, or feminine partner should sleep on the right.

Twelve

Amethyst For The Home

Amethyst purifies energy in your auric field and environment, absorbing and clearing negative energy. This helps you receive clear spiritual guidance and wisdom without being distracted.

An amethyst in the family room can help in familial bonding time, and provide the confidence and calm necessary for open communication.

Amethyst in the office will bring intuition for making tough, gut decisions in business, and stress-relief for long work days.

Placing an amethyst somewhere in the bathroom is another way to relieve anxiety during a soothing bath.

Place an amethyst, or a group of amethysts, in your home or

office to create a more peaceful environment.

Amethyst clusters and geodes are immensely popular and have amazing healing properties to rid your home and workplace from negative energy. They protect your energy and space from negativity. You can place them in the bedroom, living room, car, bathroom, or even in a meditation room to enhance positivity.

Promote a peaceful office space.
Placing amethyst in your office space can help with feelings of tension. It may help you slow your pace, so you can better concentrate on projects and get jobs done right the first time.

Place the stone near your bed or under your pillow to enjoy a better night's sleep.

By placing an amethyst geode or cluster by the front door of your home, you can better protect your home and your family. You can even do the same in your company to protect your business and the people involved with it.

Small amethyst clusters or even tumbled stones provide protection for children when you place them in their bedrooms. Setting one on their nightstand or under their pillow will help them drift off to sleep more easily and reduce bad dreams.

Place a small Amethyst tumble stone or cluster under your pillow to reduce insomnia and help you get a good night's sleep.

Placing amethyst in the kitchen will provide calmness and protection for the family. It will also encourage creativity with cooking.

Placing the amethyst under the right side of the bed where you sleep will strengthen the matriarchal energy of the mother and wife of the household.

This feng shui crystal is used in a powerful Taoist ritual to prevent your husband from having affairs with other women! The ritual involves tying a red string to the amethyst crystal and placing it under the bed, on the side that you sleep on.

So if the wife is sleeping on the right side of the bed, and wants to control the husband, then she must place an amethyst under the bed on the right side. It can be placed under the bed or tied to the foot of the bed on the right side below you—not the husband.

To hone your study skills and create improved memory and attentiveness, placing a Amethyst on your work or study desk is said to help.

Thirteen

Amethyst And Feng Shui

Fame and reputation area of your dwelling. Use its energy to give your life the boost it needs to enhance your standing in the community and within your family.

If placed in the wealth corner, amethyst can amplify the flow of prosperity into the home.

The Career & Life Journey area of the Bagua map must do with the following:

- Authenticity
- Joy
- Pursuing Your Passions
- Career-Related Choices

- Honoring Your True Self

Place an amethyst cluster or geode in this area to improve your mental concentration and meditation practice, both of which will naturally lead to an improvement in your career.

The Love & Relationships area of the Bagua map has to do with the following:

- Sensuality
- Pleasure
- Relaxation
- Receptivity
- Giving & Receiving Love
- Sexuality
- Feeling grounded amethyst opens you up to unconditional love and appreciation for others, helping us give and receive love in a healthy way.

The Family & Health area of the Bagua map has to do with the following:

- Health
- Hardiness
- Connection
- Healing the Past
- Releasing Guilt & Blame

- Connection to Ancestors
- Understanding our past lives
- Healthy Family Relationships

An amethyst cluster or geode can be placed in this area to help you overcome emotional issues related to the past.

The Wealth & Prosperity area of the Bagua map has to do with the following:

- Wealth
- Abundance
- Affluence
- Gratitude
- Luxury
- Generosity
- Allowing
- Manifestation
- Enjoyment

When you place an amethyst cluster or geode in this area of your home or workspace, you're likely to experience a deeper connection to your higher consciousness, allowing you to use your intuition better. That intuition can guide you to make better decisions that can yield greater wealth and prosperity in your life.

The Energy of Amethyst also improves our ability to manifest what we desire by allowing it to come into our lives through a calm and satisfied state of mind.

The Center & Self area of the Bagua map has to do with the following:

- Harmony
- Balance
- Feeling Safe
- Wholeness
- Empowerment
- Self-Reflection

Perhaps the most well-known attribute of the amethyst is its ability to promote calmness and serenity. Through its soothing energy, we naturally feel safe, whole, and harmonious.

The Helpful People & Travel area of the Bagua map has to do with the following:

- Giving & Receiving Help
- Guidance
- Good Connections
- Travel
- Transportation
- Ease of Technology

When you place an amethyst cluster or amethyst geode in this part of your home, office, or room, you can expect more guidance from your higher consciousness. Amethyst increases our intuition, to begin with, so placing it in this area will further enhance those benefits. You'll find it easier to get in touch with your inner spirit and the universal knowledge.

The Children & Creativity area of the Bagua map has to do with the following:

- Inner Child
- Playfulness
- Fun
- Spontaneity
- Imagination
- Unique Style
- New Ideas
- Relationships With Children & Animals

We can use amethyst in this area of the home to cleanse negative energies from our children and help them thrive. That includes your inner child, allowing you to free yourself from childhood burdens and negative experiences.

The Knowledge & Wisdom area of the Bagua map has to do with the following:

- Stillness
- Solitude
- Self-Love
- Self-Care

- Education & Study
- Meditation
- Reflection

Amethyst reduces stress, increases self-love, improves your meditation practice, and promotes healthy sleep, all associated with the Knowledge & Wisdom area.

Through the use of amethyst in this way, you will experience an increase in inner strength that carries through into every area of your life.

The Fame & Reputation area of the Bagua map has to do with the following:

- Shining Your Light
- Confidence
- Expansiveness
- Attractiveness
- Fame
- Reputation

When we place amethyst in this area, we find it helps us better understand and accept ourselves. We naturally feel more confident, which helps us share our gifts with the world.

Fourteen

Chakras

Chakras are energy points within and outside the body.

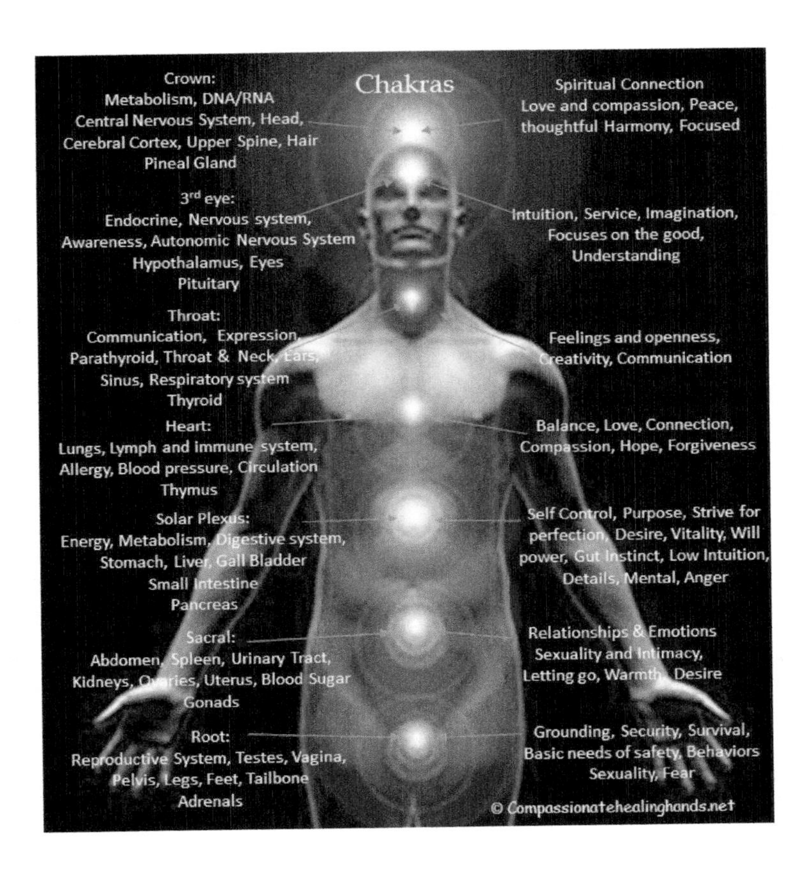

THE GAIA GATEWAY CHAKRA

WHERE IS THE GAIA GATEWAY CHAKRA

About an arm's length from your feet

This chakra takes in and processes and grounds higher vibrations. The giai gateway chakra helps protect yourself from lower energies and entity attachment.

A GOOD WORKING GIAI GATEWAY CHAKRA

You are grounded

A good working immune system

Anchor higher dimensional energies into Earth plane

You work well in everyday reality

A NOT SO GOOD WORKING GIAI GATEWAY CHAKRA

Disconnected

Oversensitive

Extreme sensitivity to earth changes, geopathic stress and electromagnetic stress

Cannot ground

EARTH STAR CHAKRA

WHERE IS THE EARTH STAR CHAKRA

The earth star chakra is 6 inches below the feet

A NOT SO GOOD WORKING EARTH STAR CHAKRA

Not grounding
- Sense of not belonging on the planet
- Feelings of helplessness
- Inability to function
- ME
- Arthritis
- Cancer
- Depression
- tiredness
- Psychiatric disturbances
- Autoimmune disease

BASE CHAKRA

WHERE IS THE BASE CHAKRA?

The base chakra is on your pubic bone, at the bottom of your spine, and also on your perineum.

A GOOD WORKING BASE CHAKRA

You feel grounded and physically energetic. You know you can take care of your basic needs – food, shelter, finances. Practical routine chores, like cleaning your home or paying bills, are a priority. Taking care of your physical body, particularly by doing enough exercise, comes naturally. You have strong links with your tribe, whether – family or friends, and they know they can rely on you.

NOT SO GOOD WORKING ROOT CHAKRA

When the root chakra is physically out of balance, the symptoms manifest themselves as lethargy, low levels of activity, low enthusiasm, and constant stimulation. You may experience lower back pain, or suffer with leg pain or immune system disorders.

When its spiritual energies are out of balance, you will feel flighty, disconnected from reality, and distant. You may begin to doubt your beliefs, stop being loyal to long-term associates and organizations, or find yourself deriving little joy from physical pleasures.

At the emotional level, the deficiencies or imbalances in the first chakra are related to:

- Excessive negativity, cynicism
- Eating disorders
- Greed
- Illusion
- Excessive feeling of insecurity, living in survival mode constantly

For a person with imbalance in the first chakra, it might be hard to feel safe in the world, and everything looks like a potential risk. The desire for security dominates and can translate into concerns about job situation, physical safety, shelter, health.

KNEE CHAKRA

WHERE IS THE KNEE CHAKRA

The knee chakra are on the knees and at the back of the knees.

A GOOD WORKING KNEE CHAKRA

The ability to move forwards with confidence
Grounding
Basic needs are fulfilled with ease

NOT SO GOOD WORKING KNEE CHAKRA

- Stiff or sore knees
- Having fear about life decisions or change
- Feeling unsure
- Resisting Change
- Issue with Kidneys
- Feeling Overwhelmed
- Knees Twinge or Collapse

SACRAL CHAKRA

WHERE IS THE SACRAL CHAKRA

The sacral chakra is 3 to 4 fingers width below the belly button, also at the back of your spine at the same height.

A GOOD WORKING SACRAL CHAKRA

When you have a clear, strong and harmonious sacral chakra, you will firstly feel comfortable in your skin. You will no longer struggle with sexual guilt or indulgence, but you'll honor your sacred sexuality and enjoy it in a balanced way. Not only will you enjoy the pleasures of life, but you will also be open to experiencing life and your passion for it. You'll be both emotionally open, but also emotionally grounded with healthy boundaries. Not only that, but you'll get back your creative flow again, and you'll enjoy the spontaneity of life.

A NOT SO GOOD WORKING SACRAL CHAKRA

When there's a problem with the Sacral Chakra, you're likely to feel bored, listless and uninspired. You may have a low sex drive, and you'll possibly feel afraid of (or resistant to) change. Physical symptoms associated with a blocked Sacral Chakra can include urinary discomfort, increased allergies and an attraction to addictive behaviors. These need not be related to drug or alcohol use. Shopping addiction, gambling, and eating issues can all be linked to issues with the Sacral Chakra.

WHAT HAPPENS WHEN YOUR SACRAL CHAKRA IS IMBALANCED

- You're addicted to anything that brings pleasure, such as food, gambling, sex, work, alcohol, drugs, compulsive buying, etc.
- You feel emotionally numb or cold, and you find it hard to feel much of any type of emotion.
- You're sexually frigid, and you have a low to non-existent libido, OR...
- You're sexually impulsive, and your libido tends to be in overdrive.
- You're neurotic, and you can't handle spontaneity or uncertainty
- You've got reproductive problems such as infertility, impotence or menstrual issues.
- You're constantly fatigued, and you have little energy for anything
- You feel inhibited and repressed from expressing your true feelings and desires, OR...
- You're extremely emotionally reactive, and you're a drama junkie
- You're emotionally hypersensitive OR emotionally aloof
- You're creatively blocked, and you tend to overthink everything
- You have lower back, kidney or stomach disorders

NAVEL CHAKRA

WHERE IS THE NAVEL CHAKRA?

On the belly button

DANTIEN CHAKRA

WHERE IS THE DANTIEN CHAKRA?

The dantien chakra is two fingers width below the belly button.

A GOOD WORKING DANTIEN CHAKRA

You are not open to manipulation from others.

A NOT SO GOOD WORKING DANTIEN CHAKRA

Energy constantly drains out from you
Project you start, but you do not finish
Chronic lethargy
No stamina
You are easily pushed around
Manipulated by others

SOLAR PLEXUS CHAKRA

WHERE IS THE SOLAR PLEXUS CHAKRA

The solar plexus area (is the upper part of the belly, where your diaphragm rests) also around your back on your spine at the same height.

Main Chakra Meanings

The main meanings associated with the third chakra are:

- Will, personal power
- Taking responsibility for one's life, taking control
- Mental abilities, the intellect
- Forming personal opinions and beliefs
- Making decisions, setting the direction
- Clarity of judgments
- Personal identity, personality
- Self-assurance, confidence
- Self-discipline
- Independence

The Solar Plexus chakra is associated with the following **psychological** and **behavioral functions**:

- Expression of will
- Intellectual abilities
- The "accounting mind" that categorizes everything, assesses the pluses and minuses in life

- Personal power
- Ability to establish ideas and plans into reality
- At higher levels, it conveys wisdom
- The main function of this energy center is to provide actual **momentum** to move forward and realize personal desires and intentions in the world. It plays a fundamental role in the development of personal power. It feeds one's **direction in life and** the actions taken to reach your goals. The solar plexus functions as the center of energy associated with ego or your self-identity. It's the seed of your personal power, self-belief, and self-worth. It fuels your intentionality, your **direction in life,** and the actions you are to take in order to reach your goals, This enables you to discover who you truly are and let your authenticity flourish. **Confidence** — The solar plexus chakra is responsible for your self-esteem and how you view yourself. It also gives you the confidence to make decisions and feel self-assured.
- **Intention & Action** — Your solar plexus chakra gives you the power to transform your thought into action.

When the **Solar Plexus chakra is balanced**, you may:

- Be assertive
- Exert your will in a way that leads to the expected results somewhat effortlessly
- Have harmonious relationships with your surrounding

A NOT SO GOOD WORKING SOLAR PLEXIS CHAKRA

Imbalances in the third chakra can manifest as:

- Excessive control and authority over your environment and people
- Or the opposite in case of deficiency or blocked energy: Feeling of helplessness, irresponsibility
- Being obsessed with minute details, seeing life through a filter of plus and minuses, while losing sight of the whole picture
- Being manipulative
- Misusing your power
- Lack of clear direction, lack of purpose or ambition
- Making plans or having many ideas without finding efficient ways to realize
- Feel powerless or victimized
- Give your power away in pursuit of validation and acknowledgment.
- Misuse your power, impose your beliefs, manipulate others to meet your interests.
- Find it difficult to take actions on your dreams.
- Have a low self-esteem
- Suffer from stomach pains and anxiety
- Imbalances of the solar plexus can also manifest in the physical body, such as fatigue, overeating, excessive weight around the stomach, and digestive system disorders such as IBS, ulcers, hypoglycemia, and diabetes.
- It can bring a lack of control in your life, as well as a loss

of identity.

- Feeling like you need to control everything and everyone around you
- Feeling helpless
- Difficulty seeing the "big picture" in life
- Lack of purpose or direction
- Dreams that lack associated plans
- Unresolved guilt about the past
- Digestive cramps
- Difficulties with short-term memory
- Bloating
- Nausea

WHEN THE SOLAR CHAKRA IS WORKING

- Have a strong sense of your own power and how to use it in healthy ways.
- Admire others with power and influence, and choose to emulate people who are
- Want to use your power and influence for good in the world?
- Trust your intuition and inner guidance
- Don't feel need in other people's confirmation and validation
- Being assertive
- Exert your will in a way that leads to the expected results somewhat effortlessly

- Have harmonious relationships with your surrounding
- anxiety
- When the solar plexus chakra is in balance, a person exudes confidence (without being arrogant), feels self-motivated, and has a sense of purpose. When out of balance, someone may suffer from low self-esteem, have trouble making decisions, and have control issues.
- A working solar plexus chakra gives you the ability to overcome fear, master your thoughts, and make conscious choices.

PALM CHAKRA

WHERE IS THE PALM CHAKRA

The palm chakra is the palm of your hands, you sense energies with the palm chakras, with your palm chakras you can manifest and actualise, you palm chakras also project energies as well

A GOOD WORKING PALM CHAKRA

Manifestation
Positive projection of energy

A NOT SO GOOD WORKING PALM CHAKRA

Negative projection of energy
Greed

The palm chakras give out and take in energy

HEART SEED CHAKRA

WHERE IS THE HEART SEED CHAKRA?

The Heart Seed Chakra is located at the breast bone

A NOT SO GOOD WORKING HEART SEED CHAKRA

Spiritually lost

This chakra governs the physical and psychic immune system, your DNA, and how you protect yourself.
Well protected
Unconditional love
forgiving
Spiritually connected

A NOT SO GOOD WORKING HIGHER HEART CHAKRA

Paranoid
Spiritually disconnected
Grieving
Needy
A psychic vampire
Immune system turns in on itself, destroying the body and its cells
There is no protection from toxins from the outside
Repeated viral and bacterial infections
ME
Epilepsy
Psoriasis
Thyroid problems

THROAT CHAKRA

The throat chakra is located in the middle of the throat and the back of the neck.

As the throat chakra governs the mouth, tongue, and neck, it relates to communication and your ability to understand and speak your inner truth. The function of the Throat chakra is driven by the principle of expression and communication. The

Throat Chakra is about the expression of yourself: Your truth, purpose in life, creativity. The Throat Chakra is connected to the way you express your life with utmost authenticity. It is about communicating your thoughts, feelings, and intentions clearly and accurately. **Key Characteristics of the Throat Chakra**

- **Expression** — This chakra is your source of creativity and expression. It empowers you to be yourself and share it with the world.
- **Truth** — The throat chakra gives you the courage to speak your truth. It is also motivated by constantly seeking truth and sharing it with others.
- **Integrity** — This chakra is the source of your personal integrity. It allows you to be honest with yourself and always stand up for what you believe in.
- **Originality** — Your fifth chakra is motivated by authenticity. It allows you to be inspired and creative, to share your ideas, and to always be authentic to yourself.
- **Communication** — The throat chakra is the center of communication. It allows you to effectively communicate your ideas and thoughts, but also has the tools to listen deeply to others around you.

The throat chakra can impact all the following:

- *Your emotional honesty*
- *Whether you live an authentic life*

- *How well do you handle conflict or confrontation?*
- *The quality of your relationships*
- *Your ability to be heard*
- *Awareness of your needs*

A NOT GOOD WORKING THROAT CHAKRA

A blocked throat chakra can contribute to feelings of insecurity, timidity, and introversion. On the other end of the spectrum, an overactive throat chakra may also lead to gossiping, nonstop talking, and being verbally aggressive or mean.

When the throat chakra has an imbalance, it can manifest as:

- Lack of control over one's speech; speaking too much or inappropriately;
- Not being able to listen to others
- Excessive fear of speaking
- Small, imperceptible voice
- Not being able to keep secrets, to keep your word
- Telling lies
- On the opposite side, a closed throat chakra might manifest as excessive secretiveness or shyness.
- Lack of connection with a vocation or purpose in life.
- Difficulty saying what you want to
- Lacking the vocabulary to describe your emotions
- Feeling like you're holding onto too many secrets
- A sense that people don't know the "real you"

Here are some signs to watch out for:

- You find it hard to express your emotions in a healthy way.
- You struggle to verbalize your thoughts.
- You feel nervous when trying to share your opinions, OR…
- You tend to aggressively push your opinions onto others.
- You struggle a lot with miscommunication in your relationships.
- You constantly feel ignored or misunderstood by others.
- You keep many secrets from others for fear of not being accepted.
- You feel anxious in conversations
- You are shy around others
- You find it hard to be your authentic self
- You tend to be over-opinionated, OR
- You struggle to have a voice of your own
- You feel almost paralyzed when doing public speaking.
- You often enter restrictive relationships that don't allow you to voice your thoughts and feelings without getting criticized.
- You find it difficult to be honest with yourself and others.
- Your actions go against your words
- You have swollen lymph nodes in your neck
- Your voice frequently cracks or sounds thin
- You suffer from hypo- or hyperthyroidism
- You have ear problems, like premature hearing loss or infections.
- You develop regular sinus, throat or upper respiratory infections
- Introverted
- Insecure

- Fear of Speaking Up
- Small Voice
- Timid
- Gossiping
- Overly Critical
- Arrogance
- Condescending
- Rude
- Inability to Listen

Meanwhile, **physical problems** caused by a misaligned throat chakra can include one or more of the following:

- A sore throat
- Erratic fluctuations in hormone levels
- A stiff or achy neck

THIRD EYE CHAKRA

WHERE IS THE THIRD EYE CHAKRA

The third eye chakra is between the eyebrows.

The third eye chakra is associated with the following psychological and behavioral characteristics:

- Vision
- Intuition
- Perception of subtle dimensions and movements of energy
- Psychic abilities related to clairvoyance and clairaudience, especially
- Access to mystical states, illumination
- Connection to wisdom, insight
- Motivates inspiration and creativity
- *Your ability to form accurate gut feelings.*
- *Your sense of the bigger picture in life.*
- *Whether you meet goals related to your deepest purpose.*
- *Balancing emotion and reason.*
- *Whether you feel stagnant or moving forward*

Correlates to our mental abilities, psychological skills, and how we evaluate beliefs and attitudes.

A NOT SO GOOD WORKING THIRD EYE CHAKRA

When the Third Eye Chakra has an imbalance, it can manifest as:

- Feeling stuck in the daily grind without being able to look beyond your problems and set a guiding vision for yourself
- Overactive third chakra without support from the rest of the chakra system may manifest as fantasies that appear more real than reality, indulgence in psychic fantasies and illusions

- Not being able to establish a vision for oneself and realize it
- Rejection of everything spiritual or beyond the usual
- Not being able to see the greater picture
- Lack of clarity
- Lack of faith in your purpose
- Feeling pointless
- Indecisiveness
- Finding your work or life insignificant
- Paranoia
- You rarely feel creative or inspired by anything
- You ignore listening to your intuition
- You are overly logical or overly emotional
- You become absorbed by the details but struggle to see the "bigger picture"
- You're often lost in your thoughts
- You habitually escape into daydreaming to avoid reality
- You are egotistically attached to special "powers" (ability to see visions, clairsentience, etc.)
- You are emotionally reactive and get upset easily
- You're addicted to external things which you believe will make you happy (relationships, food, sex, money, status, shopping, etc.)
- You struggle to see reality clearly
- You can't seem to connect to your deeper self or Soul
- Your interactions with other people are very trivial or superficial
- You mistrust or dislike people easily
- You have rigid opinions about the world that you aren't willing to change
- You are stubborn

- You find it hard to be open-minded
- You might be perceived as arrogant and opinionated
- You might be perceived as being dreamy and ungrounded
- You suffer from frequent headaches or migraines
- You have a dense and heavy ego
- You're strongly attached to outcomes
- You lack focus and decisiveness
- You suffer from vision problems and sinus issues
- You suffer from delusions/mental illness

Third eye blockages can also trigger a range of troublesome physical symptoms. The most frequently reported include:

- Headaches (including migraines)
- Eye discomfort
- Back and leg pain
- Sinus pain

SOMA CHAKRA

WHERE IS THE SOMA CHAKRA

The soma chakra is above the third eye chakra on the hair line

A GOOD WORKING SOMA CHAKRA

Deeply spiritual
Grounded

A NOT SO GOOD WORKING SOMA CHAKRA

Delusions
Out of body experiences
The soul cannot go home

CROWN CHAKRA

The Crown Chakra is our connector to the divine and our spiritual nature. It also allows for spirituality to integrate into our physical lives.

The seventh chakra influences the major body systems: the central nervous, muscular, and skin.

On an emotional level, the Crown Chakra generates devotion, inspirational and prophetic thought, mystical connections and transcendental ideas.

The more people who can connect with the power of this chakra, the more it will shift our collective consciousness on a massive scale towards a more holistic understanding of health.

A GOOD WORKING CROWN CHAKRA

- I am part of the Divine
- I honor the Divine within me
- I seek to understand and to learn from my life experiences
- I cherish my spirit
- I seek experiences that nourish my spirit
- I listen to the wisdom of universe
- I trust my intuition
- I am open to letting go of my attachments
- I live in the present moment
- I am grateful for all the goodness in my life
- I love and accept myself
- I know that all is well in my world
- I am connected with the wisdom of the universe
- I am open to divine wisdom
- My life moves with grace
- I am at peace
- I am constantly connected to my highest self."
- "We are all on this earth to make a difference."
- "I am attuned to the divine energy of the universe."
- "I know my own spiritual truth and I live in accordance with it."
- "Today I am open to divine guidance."
- "I see the beauty in the world and I embrace it."
- "Lovingly, I emit light that attracts others who will bring love into my life."
- "I am love, I am light, and I am joy."
- "I am at one with the world around me."
- "Right now, I am confident, happy and sure of my worth

A NOT SO GOOD CROWN CHAKRA

Unable to see the bigger picture
Lack of motivation
Illusions
lack of awareness and mindfulness
more serious physical disease
Dementia
Schizophrenia
Epilepsy
Headaches
Light sensitivity
Autoimmune disorders
Neurological disorders
Effects health of brain
All aspects of Mental, physical and spiritual health
Mental Fog
Learning problems
Excess interest or admiration of oneself and ones physical appearance
Depression
Sleep disorders
Endocrine system issues
Personality disorder
Mental breakdown

THE ALTA MAJOR CHAKRA

WHERE IS THE ALTA MAJOR CHAKRA

The Alta Major Chakra is inside the skull

The Alta Major Chakra is an anchor for the multidimensional light body and it gives you the bigger picture

A NOT SO GOOD WORKING ALTA MAJOR CHAKRA

Paranoid delusions which feels like reality
- Inner sight cannot open
- Ancestral disease
- Karmic disease
- Metabolic dysfunction
- Eye problems
- Cataracts
- Migraine
- Headaches
- Memory loss
- Alzheimer's
- Dementia
- Feelings of confusion
- Depression
- Dizziness
- Loss of purpose
- Spiritual depression
- Fear
- Terror

PAST LIFE CHAKRA

WHERE IS THE PAST LIFE CHAKRA

On the bony ridge on the back of the ear.

The past life chakra is where you store your past life memories and ingrained soul programs, and emotional baggage from the past.

A NOT SO GOOD WORKING PAST LIFE CHAKRA

No filter and no understanding of what the past is and what is the present.

Past life constantly impinge on the present to the extent that there maybe emotional or psychiatric disturbances.

Emotional baggage

Unfinished business

Overwhelmed by past life memories of trauma, violent death and fears.

Stuck in the past and cannot move forwards

Repeating your own past life

Recreating ancestral patterns that have been past down through family.

chronic illness

genetic or physical malfunctions

psychosomatic illness

THE SOUL STAR CHAKRA

This chakra is where your soul lives and this is the chakra

where you can heal your soul.

WHERE IS THE SOUL STAR CHAKRA

The soul star chakra is 6 inches above the head

A NOT SO GOOD WORKING SOUL STAR CHAKRA

Spiritual arrogance
Soul fragmentation
Psychological and psychiatric
Schizophrenia
Paranoia
Bipolar disorders

THE STELLAR GATEWAY CHAKRA

The stellar gateway chakra is a portal for other dimensions and other realms.

WHERE IS THE STELLAR GATEWAY CHAKRA

The stellar Gateway Chakra is 12 inches above the head

A NOT SO GOOD WORKING STELLAR GATEWAY CHAKRA

Disinformation
Illusions
Delusions
Deception
Unable to function in the everyday world
Unable to connect to the soul or higher dimensions

ATOMIC DOORWAY CHAKRA

This is the gateway to other universes, to the Akashic records of everything that ever was and will be, and to one's spirit guides.

WHERE IS THE ATOMIC DOORWAY CHAKRA

The atomic doorway chakra is 41cm above your head.

THE CAUSAL VORTEX CHAKRA

WHERE IS THE CAUSAL VORTEX CHAKRA

The Causal Vortex Chakra
Is 4 inches at the back of the head

The Causal vortex Chakra is like a universal and cosmic World Wide Web, you can heal the Etheric and Karmic blueprint in this Chakra

A NOT SO GOOD WORKING CAUSAL VORTEX CHAKRA

Ancestral and Karmic manifests as physical conditions

Fifteen

Balancing The Chakras

Chakras are vital energy centers that can be found along the spine. They connect your body, organs, mind, and spirit.

Chakras are both transmitters and receptors, meaning the frequency at which you emit energy will match the frequency of what you receive in your life, When they, the chakras are balanced, they are operating at the highest frequency and will attract people, abundance, and opportunities that you have labeled high frequency, which is wealth, prosperity and abundance.

If your chakras are not flowing and balanced, the imbalance can show as physical, emotional, or spiritual symptoms that even affect circumstances outside of yourself in your life. If your life feels out of whack, so will your chakras. Balancing your chakras benefits your mind, brain, body, soul, life and lifestyle.

When they become blocked or out of balance, you can feel discomforts, pains, or tensions, or you can experience problems in different areas of your life.

Chakras can get blocked and prevent the energy from flowing freely in and out of your body. Your life is likely to get out of balance.

When you balance your chakras, you also clear away the low vibration energies and negativity.

Everyone benefits from balancing their chakras, including infants, young children and teenagers. You also have a good ability to heal your physical, emotional, psychological, and spiritual issues.

When healing the chakras start with healing the crown chakra first.

And look up what i have written in this book, and look up the symptoms here to find out which chakra to place your Amethyst crystal.

CROWN CHAKRA

The crown chakra is the seventh chakra. Located at the top of the head.

The Crown chakra is primarily associated with the pituitary gland, and secondarily to the pineal and the hypothalamus. The hypothalamus and pituitary gland work in pair to regulate the endocrine system. Because of its location, the crown chakra is closely associated with the brain and whole nervous system. Some describe this chakra as the gateway to the cosmic self or the divine self, to universal consciousness. It's linked to the infinite, the universal. It is the gateway to spiritual wisdom. It also connects the individual to the wider universe, helping each person feel their connection to the universal energy. The crown chakra connects us with the universe and the Divine source of creation. When we realize that everything is interconnected and that we are part of the larger scheme of life, we begin to live with gratitude, faith and trust, rather than filled with fear and anxiety.

Organs and functions connected to the Crown Chakra – Head, brain, ears, eyes, pineal gland, skeletal and muscular systems, as well as the skin.

Behavioral characteristics of the Crown chakra

The crown chakra is associated with the following psychological and behavioral characteristics:

- Consciousness
- Awareness of higher consciousness, wisdom, of what is

sacred

- Connection with the formless, the limitless
- Realization, liberation from limiting patterns
- Communion with higher states of consciousness
- Ecstasy, bliss
- Presence
- devotion
- inspirational
- Prophetic thought
- Mystical connections
- Transcendental ideas
- *How much beauty you can see in the world around you*
- *Your excitement levels*
- *Motivation to reach goals*
- *Whether you have restful sleep*
- *Your ability to find peace*
- *Your self-worth*
- Notice the Beauty — The crown chakra allows you to see the beauty and divinity in all things.
- Unity — The crown chakra represents your connection to the universe. You can experience unity with everyone and everything around you.
- Awareness — This chakra brings your consciousness to a higher level, allowing your awareness to be transcendent.
- Enlightenment — The crown chakra is the gateway between the physical and cosmic self. This gives you the ability to have the utmost clarity and enlightened wisdom.
- Serenity & Bliss — The crown chakra brings feelings of serenity, joy, and deep peace about life.

Crown chakra imbalance

When the Crown chakra has an imbalance, it can manifest as:

- Being disconnected to spirit, constant cynicism regarding what is sacred
- On the opposite side, an over active crown chakra could manifest as a disconnection with the body.
- Living in your head, being disconnected from your body and earthly matters
- Obsessive attachment to spiritual matters
- Closed-mindedness
- Can limit spiritual growth
- Cause isolation
- Emotional distress.
- Isolation and loneliness; inability to connect with others
- Lack of direction
- Inability to set or maintain goals
- Feeling disconnected spiritually
- Neurological disorders
- Nerve pain
- Thyroid and pineal gland disorders
- Alzheimer's
- Recurring headaches, migraines
- Schizophrenia and delusional disorders
- Insomnia
- Depression
- Skin issues
- rashes
- acne
- eczema

- narrow-minded
- Unable to see the bigger picture
- Lack motivation
- Blame others for their crisis or stagnation.
- disillusioned
- bored
- melancholy
- restless
- Cynicism
- Apathy
- Disconnecting from your spirituality
- Self-destructive
- Confusion about what you want to do
- Lack of inspiration
- Desire to oversleep
- Poor coordination
- Chronic tension headaches
- Exhaustion
- depression
- headaches
- Neurological issues
- Parkinson's disease
- Alzheimer's
- paralysis
- epilepsy
- Multiple sclerosis
- senility
- dementia
- psychosis
- secretive
- obsessive

- critical
- wasteful
- greedy
- uncaring
- selfish
- hypocritical
- indecisiveness
- fatigue
- a sense of not belonging
- loneliness
- meaninglessness
- Psychological imbalances
- Split personalities
- Memory disorders
- Excessive gullibility
- nightmares
- cancer
- epilepsy
- baldness
- headaches
- migraine
- depression
- Alzheimer's disease
- Brain tumors
- coma
- delusions
- amnesia
- Pituitary problems
- Parkinson's disease
- hysteria
- Apathy

- Lack of care and compassion towards others
- Excessive egotism
- Insomnia
- Nightmares/night terror
- boredom with life
- Feeling of alienation from others
- Narrow-mindedness/dogmatism
- Existential depression
- Spiritual disconnection
- Rigid and limiting self-identity
- Greed and materialism
- Lack of purpose and direction
- Mental fog/confusion
- Loneliness
- Chronic fatique
- Headaches/migraines
- Light sensitivity
- Mental illnesses that involve delusions (e.g. schizophrenia)
- Neurological and endocrine disorders
- Lack of inspiration
- Greed
- Materialistic
- Lack of Empathy
- Apathy
- Sense of Elitism
- Superiority
- Disconnected From Your Body and Earthly Matters

THIRD EYE CHAKRA

The third eye chakra is the sixth chakra. Located on the forehead, between the eyebrows. The third eye chakra is most commonly represented with the color purple or bluish purple.

The third eye chakra is associated with the following psychological and behavioral characteristics:

- Vision
- Intuition
- Perception of subtle dimensions and movements of energy
- Psychic abilities related to clairvoyance and clairaudience, especially
- Access to mystical states, illumination
- Connection to wisdom, insight
- Motivates inspiration and creativity
- Mental abilities
- Psychological skills
- How we evaluate beliefs and attitudes
- The gift of this chakra is seeing - both inner and outer worlds
- Both hemispheres of the brain function in synchrony. The right hemisphere's creativity and synthetic thinking is integrated and balanced with the left hemisphere's logical and analytical thinking
- *Your ability to form accurate gut feelings.*
- *Your sense of the bigger picture in life.*
- *Whether you meet goals related to your deepest purpose.*

- *Balancing emotion and reason.*
- *Whether you feel stagnant or moving forward*
- Developing heightened intuition
- Psychic knowing
- clairvoyance
- Psychic vision
- clairaudience
- Psychic hearing
- Inner knowledge
- inspiration
- Finding your purpose for being here.

Third eye chakra imbalance

When the Third Eye Chakra has an imbalance, it can manifest as:

- Feeling stuck in the daily grind without being able to see beyond your problems and set a guiding vision for yourself.
- Overactive third chakra without support from the rest of the chakra system may manifest as fantasies that appear more real than reality, indulgence in psychic fantasies and illusions
- Not being able to establish a vision for oneself and realize it
- Rejection of everything spiritual or beyond the usual
- Not being able to see the greater picture

- Lack of clarity
- Sleep disorders
- headaches
- nightmares
- Severe depression
- Spiritual arrogance.
- Lack of faith in your purpose
- Feeling pointless
- Indecisiveness
- Finding your work or life insignificant
- Paranoia
- Headaches (including migraines)
- Eye discomfort
- Back and leg pain
- Sinus pain
- **closed-mindedness**
- **cynicism**
- **anxiety**
- **depression**
- **paranoia**
- **Various other mental illnesses**
- **Mood disorders**
- You rarely feel creative or inspired by anything
- You ignore listening to your intuition
- You are overly logical or overly emotional
- You become absorbed by the details, but struggle to see the "bigger picture".
- You're often lost in your thoughts
- You habitually escape into daydreaming to avoid reality
- You are egotistically attached to special "powers" (ability to see visions, clairsentience, etc.)

- You are emotionally reactive and get upset easily
- You're addicted to external things which you believe will make you happy (relationships, food, sex, money, status, shopping, etc.)
- You struggle to see reality clearly
- You can't seem to connect to your deeper self or soul
- Your interactions with other people are trivial or superficial.
- You mistrust or dislike people easily
- You have rigid opinions about the world that you aren't willing to change.
- You are stubborn
- You find it hard to be open-minded
- You might be perceived as arrogant and opinionated, OR...
- You might be perceived as dreamy and ungrounded
- You suffer from frequent headaches or migraines.
- You have a dense and heavy ego
- You're strongly attached to outcomes
- You lack focus and decisiveness
- You suffer from vision problems and sinus issues
- You suffer from delusions/mental illness
- **dreaminess**
- **ungroundedness**
- **Mental confusion**
- **narrow-mindedness**
- **cynicism**
- **arrogance**
- Intuition or psychic abilities may feel drained or reduced
- Headaches
- Hormone imbalances
- nightmares

- indecision
- burnout
- lack of purpose
- Trusting your inner voice
- Recalling important facts, or learning new skills
- Issues concentrating
- Sleep disturbances
- Mental fog
- confusion
- Finding yourself often thinking back over and over on situations
- Having alcohol or drugs addictions.
- A tendency to be erratic in your behavior.
- Finding it hard to be open-minded.
- Being overly logical or overly emotional.
- Not remembering the dreams.
- Feeling cut off from your internal vision and life purpose.
- Feeling like you are a victim of your life experience.
- Need to external stimulants to keep going (i.e. caffeine)
- Mistrusting, or dislike people easily.
- Trouble sleeping or insomnia
- Confusion or anxiety about decisions you need to make
- Lack of imagination
- Unsure of what to do with your life
- Poor memory
- Feel pulled to be in silence

HEART CHAKRA

The **heart chakra**, colors our life with compassion, love, and beauty.

Location: In the center of the chest (the energy center is not located where our actual heart organ lies; rather, the heart chakra is in the center of the chest area). and it is

The Heart chakra is associated with the following psychological and behavioral characteristics:

- Capacity to love
- Integration, bridge between earthly and spiritual aspirations
- Transcending personal identity and limitations of the ego
- Experience of unconditional love and connection with all
- Heart-centered discernment
- Appreciation of beauty in all things
- Experiencing deep and meaningful relationships
- One's senses of trust
- fearlessness
- peace
- generosity
- gratitude
- connectedness
- As well as change and transformation
- Healthy boundaries
- Depth in relationships with others
- Emotional control
- Love for oneself
- Self-love
- connectedness

- Are comfortable in your relationships
- Give and receive love easily
- Feel a heartfelt sense of gratitude for how wonderful your life is
- Appreciate others and feel compassion for yourself and others, without feeling sorry for anyone.
- Love yourself unconditionally

The main functions associated with the heart chakra are:

- Love for oneself and others
- Relating, relationships
- Compassion, empathy
- Forgiveness, acceptance
- Transformation, change
- Ability to grieve and reach peace
- Compassionate discernment
- Center of awareness, integration of insights

When the heart chakra is healed, you will feel being deeply connected, the harmonious exchange of energy with all that is around you, and the appreciation of beauty.

The heart chakra is associated with the **cardiac system** and the **lungs**. These organs are interdependent and rely on air and breathing to function properly.

Symptoms of a blocked heart chakra

- Difficulty in relating with others,
- Excessive jealousy
- codependency
- Being closed down
- withdrawn
- Being overly defensive
- Feeling closed down
- Jealousy; fear of intimacy
- Codependency, relying on other's approval and attention, trying to please at all costs
- Always putting oneself in the role of the savior or the rescuer; or on the contrary, falling into victimization
- Excessive isolation, being reclusive, antisocial
- Holding grudges, not being to forgive
- Respiratory ailments
- like lung infection
- bronchitis
- Circulatory issues
- Heart-related issues
- You may find it hard to develop and keep healthy relationships.
- You may tend to isolate yourself excessively
- You feel lonely
- You hold grudges against people you love
- You frequently feel jealous
- You're overly defensive
- You fear intimacy
- You put yourself in the role of the rescuer or victim
- You find it difficult to trust others
- . One might feel hard-hearted
- brokenhearted

- unhappy
- insecure
- Easily hurt
- Unable to receive love
- bitter
- resentment
- Manipulative behaviors
- Shyness
- Loneliness
- Depression/Anxiety
- Finding it hard to forgive
- Finding it hard to feel empathy
- Dependence on others for fulfillment
- jealousy
- High expectations of others
- Harsh judgment of other people
- Needing acceptance of others
- A lowered immune system (colds, flu, infections), heart and lung issues (heart palpitations common).
- Poor circulation
- High/low blood pressure
- Respiratory and breathing difficulties
- Commitment issues
- Procrastination in relationships
- shyness
- Bottled up emotions
- Trust issues
- Holding on to grudges
- Dwelling on past relationships
- Holding on to past hurts
- stressed

- anxious
- Pushing others away
- Putting yourself last
- Portraying pessimistic behaviors
- spite
- mistrust
- hatred
- unsettled
- depressed
- worried
- envy
- Asthma
- Upper back and shoulder problems
- Arm and wrist pain
- Over-loving to the point of suffocation
- Constant fear of being alone
- Shyness and social anxiety
- Being overly critical towards yourself and others
- Inability to give or receive freely
- Suspicion and fear, especially in friendships and romantic relationships
- Fear of commitment and feeling like you have to please others to be loved
- Hurt from past relationships and now feel like you have to guard yourself against being hurt again.
- Trouble with giving, receiving love, and being compassionate

THROAT CHAKRA

The location for the fifth chakra is at the level of the throat, front of neck and back of neck. This chakra is the color blue.

The Throat chakra is associated with the pharyngeal and bronchial plexi and is connected to the mouth, jaws, tongue, pharynx and palate. It's also linked to the shoulders and the neck. The gland associated with the fifth chakra is the thyroid, which regulates the processing of energy in the body through temperature, growth, and in large parts, metabolism.

The Throat chakra is associated with the following

- Expression, in particular ability to express your truth, to speak out
- Communication, whether it's verbal or non-verbal, external or internal
- Connection with the etheric realm, the subtler realms of spirit and intuitive abilities
- Propensity to create, project ideas and blueprints into reality
- Realizing your vocation, purpose
- Good sense of timing
- The Throat chakra is about the expression of yourself: Your truth, purpose in life, creativity.
- It relates to communication and your ability to understand and speak your inner truth "purely".

- Fifth chakra is to speak, listen, and express yourself from a higher form of communication.
- It is about communicating your thoughts, feelings, and intentions clearly and accurately.

The throat chakra can impact all the following:

- *Your emotional honesty*
- *Whether you live an authentic life*
- *How well you handle conflict or confrontation?*
- *The quality of your relationships*
- *Your ability to be heard*
- *Awareness of your needs*

WHEN THE THROAT CHAKRA IS IN BALANCE

We speak, listen, and express ourselves openly and authentically.

IMBALANCES IN THE THROAT CHAKRA CAN LEAD TO

Feelings of insecurity
timidity
introversion
gossiping
Nonstop talking

Being verbally aggressive
mean

- Lack of control over one's speech; speaking too much or inappropriately;
- Not being able to listen to others
- Excessive fear of speaking
- Small, imperceptible voice
- Not being able to keep secrets, to keep your word
- Telling lies
- On the opposite side, a closed throat chakra might manifest as excessive secretiveness or shyness.
- Lack of connection with a vocation or purpose in life.
- One has difficulty staying true to themselves
- Has difficulty expressing needs, desires, and opinions with themselves and others.
- Difficulty tuning in to the true self
- The urge to hide opinions
- Hide desires from yourself and others
- Dominating conversations
- Difficulty listening to others
- Neck pain
- Hormone fluctuation (relating to the thyroid)
- We ignore our inner voice
- Feel afraid of expressing ourselves
- Have trouble listening to others.
- a sore throat
- Neck and shoulder pain
- arrogance
- timidity
- fear

- Manipulative behavior
- Thyroid imbalances
- Hearing problems
- tonsillitis
- Mouth ulcers
- tinnitus
- bronchitis
- asthma
- Ear infections
- Difficulty expressing your thoughts
- Feeling timid or shy
- Talking without thinking
- dishonesty
- insensitivity
- insecurity
- Social anxiety
- Difficulty making sound decisions
- Jaw pain
- hoarseness
- Dental disorders
- earache
- Hearing issues
- Difficulty saying what you want to
- Lacking the vocabulary to describe your emotions
- Feeling like you're holding onto too many secrets
- A sense that people don't know the "real you"

SOLAR PLEXUS CHAKRA LOCATION

The solar plexus area is the upper part of the belly, where your diaphragm rests.

The main meanings associated with the third chakra are:

- Will, personal power
- Taking responsibility for one's life, taking control
- Mental abilities, the intellect
- Forming personal opinions and beliefs
- Making decisions, setting the direction
- Clarity of judgments
- Personal identity, personality
- Self-assurance, confidence
- Self-discipline
- Independence
- Governs our personal power, our ability to handle stress, and our feeling of inner knowing

Key Characteristics of the Solar Plexus Chakra

- **Identity** — As the core of your personality and identity, the solar plexus chakra allows you to bloom into your authentic self and discover who you truly are.
- **Personal Power** — The solar plexus chakra is the source of your personal power. This empowers you to take control of your thoughts, emotions, and actions.
- **Willpower** — Working with your personal power, your solar plexus chakra gives you the willpower and self-discipline to get things done.
- **Confidence** — The solar plexus chakra is responsible for

your self-esteem and how you view yourself. It also gives you the confidence to make decisions and feel self-assured.
- **Intention & Action** — Your solar plexus chakra gives you the power to transform your thought into action.

The Solar Plexus chakra is associated with the following **psychological** and **behavioral functions**:

- Expression of will
- Intellectual abilities
- The "accounting mind" that categorizes everything, assesses the pluses and minuses in life
- Personal power
- Ability to establish ideas and plans into reality
- At higher levels, it conveys wisdom
- The solar plexus is the center of energy associated with ego or your self-identity. It's the seed of your personal power, self-belief, and self-worth.
- The core of our personality, our identity, of our ego

The main function of this energy center is to provide actual **momentum** to move forward and realize personal desires and intentions in the world. It plays a fundamental role in the development of personal power. It feeds one's direction in life and the actions taken to reach your goals. It influences preoccupations about social status and self-image. This chakra is connected to our sense of sight.

It governs our ability to achieve the goals we set for ourselves, moderates our self-esteem, oversees our raw emotions, and we draw on it for our self-discipline. When the energy of our Solar Plexus is balanced, our outlook on life improves, criticisms and problems are easier to handle, and you have control over your emotions and thoughts. The ego is easier to handle. You will understand and accept your inner peace, and radiate that acceptance outward, coming to appreciate people and things around you. When balanced, our Solar Plexus gives us confidence in ourselves and our performance. We feel accomplished and proud of our work and achieving our goals. We create an emotional focal point. The Solar Plexus Chakra is connected to the sense of sight. The Solar Plexus helps with mental clarity as well as learning new things, it is the home of our power, self-esteem, self-image, energy, will, responsibility, and life purpose.

When the **Solar Plexus chakra is balanced**, you may:

- Be assertive
- Exert your will in a way that leads to the expected results somewhat effortlessly
- Have harmonious relationships with your surrounding
- Have a strong sense of your own power and how to use it in healthy ways.
- Admire others with power and influence, and choose to emulate people who are
- Want to use your power and influence for good in the world?

- Trust your intuition and inner guidance
- Don't feel need in other people's confirmation and validation
- Being assertive
- Exert your will in a way that leads to the expected results somewhat effortlessly
- Have harmonious relationships with your surrounding
- Confident
- motivated
- purposeful
- reliable
- Gives you the ability to overcome fear
- Master your thoughts
- Make conscious choices
- When balanced, our Solar Plexus gives us confidence in ourselves and our performance. We feel accomplished and proud of our work and achieving our goals.
- You are clear on your purpose in life and take a healthy responsibility for your direction in life.
- We feel happy and grounded in our lives and will experience life as it should be, without pain, hardships or illness.
- Balance the solar plexus chakra will mean releasing any unresolved shame in your being.
- Balance here will allow you to take positive steps in the right direction at all times, enable calculated risk taking, and a spontaneity and playfulness to life.

SACRAL CHAKRA

The sacral chakra is the second chakra. It is associated with the emotional subtle body. The second chakra is the center of feeling, emotion, pleasure, sensuality, intimacy, connection and creativity.

The second chakra shifts from obeying tribal, family authority, and allows us to discover satisfying relationships and interests of our own. The sacral chakra's main focus is to allow the individual to discover what they enjoy, to form hobbies, create loving and exciting relationships, and even creativity in lovemaking and sexual eroticism.

Sacral chakra location

The most common location for the sacral chakra is about three inches below the navel, at the center of your lower belly. In the back, it's located at the same point in the back.

Behavior characteristics of the sacral chakra

The sacral chakra is associated with the following psychological and behavior functions:

- Emotions, feelings
- Relationships, relating
- Expression of sexuality, sensual pleasure
- Feeling the outer and inner worlds
- Creativity
- Fantasies

The sacral chakra is associated with the realm of emotions.

It's the center of our feelings and sensations. It's particularly active in our sexuality and the expression of our sensual and sexual desires. The energy of this chakra allows you to let go, move, and feel change and transformation occurring within your body. It allows you to experience this moment as it is, in its own fullness. A person with a strong second chakra can survive financially and physically on his or her own, and bond with others to form harmonious friendships. A balanced second chakra can take risks and have the resilience to recover when things go wrong. The sacral chakra has the power to utilize your talent and actualize the life you want to live.

NOT SO GOOD WORKING SACRAL CHAKRA

- Dependency, co-dependency with other people or a substance that gives you easy access to pleasure
- Being ruled by your emotions
- The opposite: Feeling numb, out of touch with yourself and how you feel
- Overindulgence in fantasies, sexual obsessions
- Or the opposite: Lack of sexual desire or satisfaction
- Feeling stuck in a particular feeling or mood
- Abusive, controlling relationships
- Cause bullying in the workplace
- Fear of abandonment
- Loss of financial and creative power.
- Chronic lower back pain

- Arthritis
- Genital or sexual problems
- Hip issues
- Low confidence,
- lack of motivation,
- Inability to create intimate connections with others,
- lack of interest in self-expression
- lack of interest artistic abilities,
- infertility
- Urinary problems
- Difficulties giving birth
- Difficulties producing orgasms
- a low libido
- depression
- detachment
- indulgent
- aggressive
- Over sensitive
- fear
- anxiety
- Poor boundaries
- anemia
- hypoglycemia
- Lower back pain
- Joint problems
- Low energy
- Spleen and kidney issues
- Premenstrual syndrome
- You're likely to feel bored, listless and uninspired
- Shopping addiction
- gambling

- Issues with eating
- Resistance to change
- Person feels shameful
- Sexually dysfunctional
- Prone to addictions
- Compulsive behaviors
- infertility
- impotence
- Menstrual issues
- Lower back, kidney, or stomach disorders.

When healing with healing crystals, read through the chakra's information in this book, and which ever symptom you have, get a healing crystal that heals that symptom and puts the healing crystal on that chakra. The best books for crystals for symptoms are Judy Hall Crystal Prescription books, but place crystals for the symptom of the chakra that I have stated.

SACRAL CHAKRA

The sacral chakra is the second chakra. It is associated with the emotional subtle body. The second chakra is the center of feeling, emotion, pleasure, sensuality, intimacy, connection and creativity.

The second chakra shifts from obeying tribal, family authority, and allows us to discover satisfying relationships and interests of our own. The sacral chakra's focus is to allow the individual to discover what they enjoy, to form hobbies, create loving and exciting relationships, and even creativity in lovemaking and sexual eroticism.

Sacral chakra location

The most common location for the sacral chakra is about three inches below the navel, at the center of your lower belly. In the back, it's located at the same point in the back.

Behavior characteristics of the sacral chakra

The sacral chakra is associated with the following psychological and behavior functions:

- Emotions, feelings
- Relationships, relating
- Expression of sexuality, sensual pleasure
- Feeling the outer and inner worlds
- Creativity
- Fantasies

The sacral chakra is associated with the realm of emotions. It's the center of our feelings and sensations. It's particularly active in our sexuality and the expression of our sensual and sexual desires. The energy of this chakra allows you to let go, move, and feel change and transformation occurring within your body. It allows you to experience this moment as it is, in its own fullness. A person with a strong second chakra can survive financially and physically on his or her own, and bond with others to form harmonious friendships. A balanced second chakra can take risks and have the resilience to recover when things go wrong. The sacral chakra has the power to utilize your talent and actualize the life you want to live.

NOT SO GOOD WORKING SACRAL CHAKRA

- Dependency, co-dependency with other people or a substance that gives you easy access to pleasure
- Being ruled by your emotions
- The opposite: Feeling numb, out of touch with yourself and how you feel
- Overindulgence in fantasies, sexual obsessions
- Or the opposite: Lack of sexual desire or satisfaction
- Feeling stuck in a particular feeling or mood
- Abusive, controlling relationships
- Cause bullying in the workplace
- Fear of abandonment
- Loss of financial and creative power.
- Chronic lower back pain
- Arthritis
- Genital or sexual problems
- Hip issues
- Low confidence,
- lack of motivation,
- Inability to create intimate connections with others,

- lack of interest in self-expression
- lack of interest artistic abilities,
- infertility
- Urinary problems
- Difficulties giving birth
- Difficulties producing orgasms
- a low libido
- depression
- detachment
- indulgent
- aggressive
- Over sensitive
- fear
- anxiety
- Poor boundaries
- anemia
- hypoglycemia
- Lower back pain
- Joint problems
- Low energy
- Spleen and kidney issues
- Premenstrual syndrome
- You're likely to feel bored, listless and uninspired
- Shopping addiction
- gambling
- Issues with eating
- Resistance to change
- Person feels shameful
- Sexually dysfunctional
- Prone to addictions
- Compulsive behaviors

- infertility
- impotence
- Menstrual issues
- Lower back, kidney, or stomach disorders.

When healing with healing crystals, read through the chakra's information in this book, and which ever symptom you have, get a healing crystal that heals that symptom and puts the healing crystal on that chakra. The best books for crystals for symptoms are Judy Hall Crystal Prescription books, but place crystals for the symptom of the chakra that I have stated.

BASE/ROOT CHAKRA

The Base Chakra, or Root Chakra, is called Muladhara in Sanskrit, is located at the base of the spine or pubic bone, and controls the energy for kinesthetic feeling and movement. It is the foundation of physical energy and spiritual energy for the body. The first chakra is associated with the Earth element.

The typical color used to represent the root chakra is a rich red.

The Root chakra helps ground us within our *physical bodies* and plays an important role in our daily survival.

The root chakra is linked to physical realities of life – security, shelter, sustenance, family, tribe. The first chakra is associated with primordial trust, and is the area of the etheric body where your ambitions, passion, and moving forward in life, interest in life and sex drive originates, and is the chakra associated with our basic instincts for food, shelter, sex and survival, and housing. Grounding, Support, and foundation for living our lives. You will have exploration to find your life's purpose and achieve. The root chakra regulates the energy associated with instinct, survival, and safety.

When the root chakra is imbalanced due to trauma, psychological issues, such as chronic fear, and psychosomatic suppression and repression, we experience a disruption in the flow of life. Often our blocked energy centers lead to constant personal, existential and relationship issues.

This is the root layer 1st Chakra of our Unconscious Mind, and it functions as a hard drive for the ego. In this hard drive is the cellular memory storage from all of one's life streams. This means that cellular memories from past lives, present lives and future lives may all be stored in this memory hard drive. These memories are not given value when recorded, whether they are recorded, whether one may perceive them as good or bad. These many multiple memories are stored on the root hard drive of every human being. Whether one was a fetus, baby, in between lifetimes, or unconscious when the body suffered "abuse"; it was recorded in one's memory storage whether one currently remembers that event consciously or not. Because the planet was invaded and our individual memory and identity erased from those tragic events, almost all human beings have four main areas of cellular memory record in their unconscious mind at varying degrees.

Those four main areas are: Abuse, Trauma, Shock and Devastation.

Some people will feel these painful memories, but not know what caused them or where they came from. Others will suffer from shock and have shut these memories down completely as a coping mechanism. Others are very successful in clearing these memories through emotional clearing practices, such as crystal healing

,. Since this 1D unconscious mind controls our autonomic nervous system and autonomic bodily functions, unhealed memory trauma in these four main areas creates many kinds of physical symptoms and disease.

Each chakra has specific areas of the body it governs, and this chakra ensures the function and healing of the organs in its area. These organs are the genitals and the colon, as well as the legs, joints and feet.

When the root chakra is open, we feel confident in our ability to withstand challenges and stand on our own two feet. When your Root Chakra is open, you...

Have a strong connection with your family.

Have friends that are like family to you.

Feel wanted and loved
Feel content with your body
Are confident with money
Always have enough for what you need and want
Feel safe on Earth and on your path.

If this chakra is in balance, you feel safe, secure and connected to the earth. You don't worry about money, as you know the universe always supports you, and you know that your needs are always met.

You're sexually balanced, and relationships, money, career and home situation are all manageable.

When you have a balanced root chakra, you have energy and vitality, and can easily focus on the tasks you need to do during the day. Your body will crave healthy foods that nourish and fuel it.

With a balanced root chakra, you won't have any lower body issues, and you feel great from the base of the spine down. Your bowels work great, and everything runs smoothly around your feet, legs and hips.

When the flow of energy is blocked, it disrupts physical, emotional, and mental health.

When it is physically out of balance, the symptoms manifest themselves as lethargy, low levels of activity, low enthusiasm, and constant stimulation. You may experience lower back pain, or suffer with leg pain or immune system disorders, excessive negativity, cynicism. A blockage in the root chakra prevents the release of grief, guilt, and sadness, contributing to the inability to move forward and preventing you from following your destiny.

When its spiritual energies are out of balance, you will feel flighty, disconnected from reality, and distant. You may begin to doubt your beliefs, stop being loyal to long-term associates and organizations, or find yourself deriving little joy from physical pleasures.

If we are imbalanced in this chakra, it can manifest as a lack of physicality, being underweight, spacey and anxious. Or it may manifest as excessive physicality in being overweight and overly attached to the physical by hoarding, over eating, indulgence in pleasure, or over-accumulation of stuff.

As this chakra provides our roots and foundation for the rest of the chakra system, it is vital to have the base chakra in balance.

Moving our bodies allows energy to flow again. It can trigger blockages to shift and cause accumulated energies to be released, redistributed and balanced.

Movement brings us into our physicality, brings our energy down from our heads into our roots, allowing a real connection with not only our physical selves, but also the physicality of the world around us.

Crystals with the red, brown, or black color rays help restore balance to the Base Chakra. The benefits of just a few minutes a day, with one of these crystals resting between the legs for 5 - 10 minutes.

Activities that connect you with nature, such as hiking, gardening, rock collecting, and physical outdoor games.

Many of us have sustained emotional and physical traumas in life, which may have affected the formation and flow of our chakras.

This biography of our experience is energetically recorded in our chakra system.

These energetic imprints can upset the flow of subtle energy and cause our chakras to compensate by either restricting energy flow, becoming deficient or under-active, or becoming overactive and excessive. Or even a combination of both.

Tips to balance the Base Chakra

1. Create a clean and healthy home environment, and spend as much time as possible in healthy environments, especially nature.

2. Find a form of exercise that suits you, and carry it out in a balanced way.

3. Eat healthy and ensure you get the right vitamins, minerals and nutrients for your body.

4. Learn to listen to your body's needs – know the signs when illness is coming on, or when you need to take a break etc.

5. Limit the amount of toxins you put into your body, including alcohol and drugs, but also the toxins in the food you eat, the chemicals in your cleaning products have organic etc.

Blocked Root Chakra Symptoms

A root chakra imbalance can throw your whole system out of order, leaving you feeling ungrounded and uncomfortable.

What Blocks the Root Chakra?

Childhood trauma
Poor mother-child relationship
Impatience
Financial difficulties
Poverty
Physical abuse
Physical neglect
Fear of change
Selfishness
Holding onto unexpressed emotions
trauma
experiences held in the chakra memory / cellular memory
toxins
Poor diet
lack of exercise…
Unhealthy environmental exposure
Unhealthy lifestyle choices

Some of the most common root chakra problems and symptoms include the following:

An increase in your anxiety levels

Feeling threatened or unsafe

Panic attacks or panic attack symptoms (like hyperventilation or a racing heart).

Negativity towards yourself and others

Concentration difficulties

An unhealthy relationship with food (e.g. starving, binging or purging).

Low self-confidence

Doubts about things you used to take for granted.

Trouble making decisions

Excessive reliance on external feedback

Hypochondria

Root Chakra Affirmations To Use

I have a healthy body, a healthy mind, and an abundant life.

I am secure and happy in my home.

I am stable and secure.

I nurture myself and care for my well-being.

I am confident in all that I do.

I believe in me.

I am at home, wherever I am.

I love myself.

Psychological symptoms of blockage include:

Anxiety disorders
fear
Panic attacks
worry
overthinking
depression
nightmares
Emotionally disconnected
Disconnected from the body
Anger/rage.

Physical symptoms of blockage include:
Lethargic and physically drained
Problems in the colon
Problems with the bladder, with elimination,
Issues with lower back
Left arm, leg, or feet issues
Inflammation
cramps
In men, prostate problems may occur
Eating disorders may also be a sign of a root chakra imbalance
Feeling stuck and sluggish
Stress due to over-reliance on external circumstances
Persistent financial problems
Feeling that your parents have abandoned you
Constantly getting by or going without
Hatred and anger toward your body
Feeling you are not good enough the way you are
You are nervous and anxious all the time.
You feel empty inside and disconnected from everyone

You don't think you have enough money
You are a shopaholic
You have anger issues
People tend to walk all over you
You eat too much or too little
You are afraid of change and the future
You are always tired
You have no idea who you are
Or, people influence you so easily
You wonder why your career is going nowhere.
feeling worried about basic survival needs like money, work, food and shelter.
lack of focus
co-dependency
restlessness
Feeling abandoned
sciatica
hypertension
impotence
guilt
resentment
loneliness
insecurities
Feeling ungrounded
unconfident
indecisive
anxious
addictions
phobias
obsessions
Inability to move forward and preventing you from following

your destiny

Varicose veins

constipation

diarrhea

Rectal/anal problems

impotence

Water retention

Problems with groin, hips, legs, knees, calves, ankles, and feet.

You may feel "stuck" and just can't seem to move forward in life.

Sense of emptiness

Trouble saving money

Chronic health problems

lack of healthy boundaries with others

Poor communication with the loved ones

The sensation of being out of space

The feeling of disconnection

lack of energy

Generalized fear

Materialism and greed, obsession with money

Chronic fatigue

Identity crisis

Little interest in intimate/physical relations with the partner

Linking one's sense of well-being to external factors

lack of confidence

illusion

Feeling Insecure

Operating Out of Fear

Lacking Support Systems

Obsessing About Finances

Trust Issues
Hypochondria
Lacking Authenticity
suspicious
Feeling unhappy about your health
Constantly worry about your well being
Craving comfort foods
Fear of job instability
Desire to be outside more
Inability to focus or sit still

Your sense of well-being is highly dependent upon external circumstances. So long as everything is going smoothly and to your liking, you feel OK, but when circumstances aren't to your liking, you feel insecure.

Struggling with personal relationships

Stressing to get through your daily activities/responsibilities and make ends meet.

Feel depleted
Feel hopeless
lonely
ungrounded
Degenerative arthritis
headaches
aloofness
lack of physical strength or stamina
Weak legs and knees
Lymphatic congestion
Weight gain/loss
Auto-immune disorders
Chronic fatigue syndrome
You believe the only person you can rely on is yourself.

You're a workaholic who tends to burn out easily

You have a dysfunctional relationship with your family.

You feel like there's "never enough" to go around, and you need to fight for what you want.

You're terrified of a loss of control

You are hyper-vigilant to any perceived signs of threat from others or your surroundings.

You feel dizzy, anxious, spacey, and ungrounded for most of the day.

You find it difficult and scary to be your authentic self around others.

You feel disconnected from other people and nature

You are a hoarder who likes to "collect" many things, making your living space constricted and cluttered

You binge-eat or stop eating completely when you get depressed or anxious.

You have leg and foot problems, like swelling, infection, cramps, and circulation

Feeling stuck and sluggish

When healing with healing crystals, read through the chakra's information in this book and which ever symptom you have, got a healing crystal that heals that symptom and put the healing crystal on that chakra. The best books for crystals for symptoms are Judy Hall Crystal Prescription books, but place crystals for the symptom of the chakra that i have

MAIN REASONS YOU HAVE BLOCKED CHAKRAS AND A NEGATIVE LIFE

The types of exercises you do exercises suitable for you.
The fluids and foods you consume.
The negativity you breathe in and out.
The toxic chemical you clean with.
The environment you live.
The toxins in your environment.
The weather you expose yourself too.
The books you read.
The multiple relationships you have.
The television and movies you watch.
The sexual relationships you have.
The multiple sexual relationships you have.
The words you speak and what you say.
What you listen to.
The lies you speak.
The people you associate with.
The items in your home.
The people you have in your home.
Your past, present, and future.
The clothes you wear.
The decor in your home.
Your emotions.
The way you work with your ability.
Using people for your own self-gratification.
Your thoughts.
Your family.
Your friends.
Your finances.

How you feel towards yourself.

How you feel towards others.

Where you go shopping.

The businesses and services you associate with and buy from.

Who you trust.

Not listening to yourself.

Putting others first before yourself.

What you learn and teach.

Taking credit and praise when it was not you who did the good deed or work.

Your appearance.

Your DNA.

How you breathe.

What you sell.

What you project onto others.

What others project onto you.

Your vocals.

Your crimes.

Not obeying the law.

Your photographs.

Your memories.

Not doing what's positively for yourself.

Stealing others good ideas.

Stealing.

Who you have as your friends.

Your Ancestors.

Your Mother and Father.

Your Brothers and Sisters.

Your Aunts and Uncles.

Your Grandparents.

Your cousins.

Your ex-partners.
Your children.
Who you worship.
Where you worship.
The negativity and badness you send out to others.
The colors you surround your self with.
The partner you choose to be with.
The company you work for.
The business you own.
The pregnancies you have.
The children that are born.
Not being your self.
The amount of pregnancies you have.
Who you get pregnant to.
Not doing what you want to do.
Not moving on to new.
Who your attached to.
Who your connected to.
The invisible.
Your Angels, as you feel for your angels and they feel for you too.
Spirits, you may feel for them.
Being bad and mean and negative to others.

But the good news is that you can heal and change all of these aspects in your life, and it is very very much exciting to heal and change your life and your self as when you have problems in your life then you heal and change them problems and the problem gets healed and every part of you is happier and positive and your lifestyle gets so much better to live and you start enjoying your own life. there are lots of non-fiction books that can help you change your lifestyle on smile.amazon.co.UK.

Sixteen

Chakras To Place Amethyst

Place Amethyst crystal on these chakras to heal

EARTH STAR CHAKRA
6 inches below feet

- centering
- For detoxification

WHAT IS DETOXIFICATION

Detoxification is the removal of toxic substances from a living organism, including the human body, which is mainly carried out by the liver.

BENEFITS OF DETOXIFICATION

Weight Loss and Management

Detoxing can also help with long-term weight management.

More Energy

An energy boost is one of the first benefits of detoxing you'll notice.

Aids Internal Organs

As mentioned above, detoxing helps your body out with toxin removal. It purifies toxins that your organs may not be able to keep up with, and gives those organs that are responsible for waste removal a much-needed rest.

Better Immune System

Since detoxing takes some of the workload off your organs, they can then do a better job of protecting your body from illness.

Nicer Breath

The removal of toxins from your body has some pleasant side effects besides improving your health.

One of the benefits of detoxing is better breath. Your digestive system will be able to function better, removing some of the causes of bad breath.

Clearer Skin

You can use all the most elaborate skincare regimes, but if your diet isn't healthy, you'll still experience skin problems. A detox is one of the surefire ways to clear up your skin.

Improved Thinking

For clearer thoughts and a better memory, detoxing is the way to go.

Shinier Hair

Shiny, healthy hair is yet another benefit of detoxing. Your follicles need the right nutrients to grow healthy hair. A buildup of toxins prevents those nutrients from getting where they need to be and often results in dry, brittle, broken tresses.

You might also see faster growth, making this a great idea for anyone planning to grow out their hair.

Slowed Signs of Aging

Detoxing helps you slow down the visible signs of aging by reducing toxins that contribute to the skin damage we usually associate with growing older.

- Heals geopathic stress

WHAT IS GEOPATHIC STRESS

Geopathic Stress is a generic term used to cover all the seen and unseen energy patterns around, that in most cases are detrimental. Earth energy lines, water veins, energy spirals, human created lines, ley lines and toxic lines all form a natural part of the problem. These are joined by technopathic stress, spirit lines and place memories that are caused by humans –

especially the emotional outpourings that permeate through our homes and workplaces.

What are the causes of geopathic stress

- Geopathic stress can be caused by harmful earth energies and underground water streams.
- Explosions, quarrying, tunneling etc
- New roads, railways, construction sites, deep foundations especially with steel footings, lampposts, cabling, power stations, sub-stations, water mains etc
- Military bases
- Old battle grounds and scenes of trauma
- Communication masts
- Emissions from all sources (man-made), mobiles, TVs etc
- Ring main wiring
- Energetic gridlock of the earth grids

What are the effects of Geopathic Stress

Some people are sensitive to these energies and over a period of prolonged exposure their immune system can be suppressed leading to disturbed sleep, fatigue or illness.

- Disturbed sleep
- General fatigue and lethargy
- Headaches
- Illness ranging from reoccurring cold and infections to more serious illnesses such as ME, Chronic Fatigue, depression. Cancer has also been associated with Geopathic

stress
- Nightmares
- If sitting on Geopathic stress, it may be difficult to concentrate or promote sleepiness.
- Babies and young children tend to unconsciously move way from Geopathic Stress and you will often see them if on Geopathic stress in an awkward position at one end or scrunched up at one side, trying to move away from the detrimental energy.
- Infertility and repeated miscarriages

BENEFITS OF HEALING GEOPATHIC STRESS

- Improved Sleep
- Renewed energy
- Improved health
- Ability to focus and concentrate

- For anti pollutants

WHAT ARE POLLUTANTS

A pollutant is a substance or energy introduced into the environment that has undesired effects, or adversely affects the usefulness of a resource.

BENEFITS OF HEALING POLLUTANTS

Reducing pollution at its source can have a rapid and substantial impact on health. Within a few weeks, respiratory and irritation symptoms, such as shortness of breath, cough, phlegm, and sore throat, disappear

- For sex

WHAT IS SEX

Sex can mean different things to different people. When most people talk about 'having sex' they are usually referring to sexual intercourse (or penetrative sex).

BENEFITS OF SEX

Boosts Your Libido

Longing for a more lively sex life? "Having sex will make sex better and will improve your libido.

Improves Women's Bladder Control

A strong pelvic floor is important for avoiding incontinence. Good sex is like a workout for your pelvic floor muscles. When you have an orgasm, it causes contractions in those muscles, which strengthens them.

Lowers Your Blood Pressure

Counts as Exercise

Sex is a really great form of exercise, Sex uses about five calories per minute.

Lowers Heart Attack Risk

A good sex life is good for your heart, Besides being a great way to raise your heart rate, sex helps keep your estrogen and testosterone levels in balance.

Lessens Pain

Before you reach for an aspirin try for an orgasm.

9. Improves Sleep

You may nod off more quickly after sex, and for good reason. After orgasm, the hormone prolactin is released, which is responsible for the feelings of relaxation and sleepiness" after sex.

Eases Stress

Being close to your partner can soothe stress and anxiety.

- For indigo children

WHAT ARE INDIGO CHILDREN

Indigo children are children who are believed to possess special, unusual, and sometimes supernatural traits or abilities.

- Overcome alienation

EARTH CHAKRA

Below feet

- To heal Geopathic stress

- To dispel energy

WHAT DOES DISPEL ENERGY MEAN

To make energy go away

FEET CHAKRA

on the souls of feet

KNEE CHAKRA

Behind the knees

BASE/ROOT CHAKRA

Base of your spine, and perineum, pubic bone

- centering
- Over spending
- Financial decisions
- To heal Angina

WHAT IS ANGINA

Angina is chest pain caused by reduced blood flow to the heart muscles. Angina is a warning sign that you're at a higher risk of serious problems like heart attacks or strokes.

BENEFITS OF HEALING ANGINA

Treatment can help stop angina attacks and reduce the risk of further problems like heart attacks.

- For Fatigue

WHAT IS FATIGUE

Fatigue can be described as the extreme tiredness and lack of energy and motivation (both physical and mental).

BENEFITS OF HEALING FATIGUE

More energy
More motivation
Less tiredness

- For over indulgence

WHAT DOES OVER INDULGENCE MEAN

have too much of something enjoyable, especially food or drink.

- For sluggishness

WHAT IS SLUGGISHNESS

lacking energy or alertness

Reasons You Feel Sluggish

B12 Deficiency

Also known as cobalamin, vitamin B12 is important for the production of red blood cells. It's one of the several B vitamins essential for converting your food into glucose, the preferred energy source for cells.

Imbalanced Thyroid

A sluggish thyroid translates to sluggish energy. Why? When hormones are out of balance, they can lead to confusion, weight gain, and fatique.

Hormone Imbalance

As mentioned in number two, hormone balance is the most important thing when it comes to keeping your energy levels in check. Improper levels of testosterone or estrogen, too little human growth hormone output, and not enough thyroid hormone production can intertwine and deplete your ability to think and act properly — so-called brain fog.

Your Digestion Is Off

Your energy levels have something to do with the state of your gut. It turns out that if you're not digesting the food you're eating, you're probably also not absorbing an adequate supply of their life-giving vitamins, minerals, antioxidants, and other beneficial compounds. All nutrients provide energy, either directly or indirectly, but if you're lacking the enzymes to digest foods and thus not receiving vitamins, glucose, and minerals, you're not going to be experiencing excellent energy levels.

Not Getting Enough Exercise

Exercise burns calories, lifts mood, and it also improve energy.

- For detoxification
- For chronic tiredness
- Ameliorate aggression
- Heals addictions
- Alcohol addiction
- For cravings
- To heal food, binge And comfort eating
- For gambling
- For sex
- For indigo children

WHAT ARE INDIGO CHILDREN

Also referred to as a crystal or star child, **an indigo child is a person who has come into this world destined to create change and spiritual awakened humanity.** Indigo children are considered to be freethinkers with profound insight into the human condition and an ability to see the truth clearly. As spiritually gifted old souls, indigo children find it hard to fit into mainstream society and often become misunderstood, rejected, or misdiagnosed and medicated. The indigo child is also thought to possess strong intuition and varying spiritual gifts such as the ability to communicate with spirit guides

SIGNS YOUR AN INDIGO CHILD

1. You are strong willed

You are a passionate person who will do anything it takes to accomplish your goals or dreams. Even if other people criticize or don't support you, you still keep going no matter what.

2. You're an old soul

You feel as though you've lived many lifetimes, and possess a wisdom that others your age don't yet have. As a child, you may have behaved like an old man or woman, and as an adult, you have a deeply spiritual and philosophical outlook on life.

3. You're a freethinker

No idea or belief is too holy for you to dissect or reject. You prefer to think for yourself rather than blindly following the crowd. As an indigo child, questioning is everything to you.

4. You're a headstrong nonconformist

As a child or teenager, you may have been thought of as "naughty," "obnoxious," disobedient, and contrarian. As an adult, you still cannot stand being boxed in or controlled by others. As a headstrong nonconformist, you prefer to find your own truth and forge your own path.

5. You're a passionate truth-seeker

Truth, to you, is of primary importance. You are always seeking to distinguish truth and reality from lies and deception. When you are around others, you can immediately tell when someone is lying or hiding something. Although the truth hurts, you honor it above all else. You would prefer to suffer from the truth than be happy believing lies.

7. You are highly intuitive

Your keen perception also makes you highly intuitive. You can often intuit the best course of action as well as know things about others that are secret or hidden.

8. You want to change the world

Deep in your heart, you feel a driving force to create positive change on this planet.

9. You're empathetic and compassionate

You care so much about this planet and other people that it often hurts. Every time you see or hear of violence, destruction, and cruelty, you feel sorrow and anger. Your high level of empathy and compassion means that you often struggle with anxiety or depression.

10. You have a loner/autonomous personality

As a free spirit you don't like to be held down by anyone or anything. You find it difficult to be around too many people at once, and often prefer to spend time in your own company. As a lover of autonomy, you enjoy solitude and the insight it can bring.

11. You're highly creative

Your nonconformist brain loves to express itself through art and creativity. Whether it be drawing, dancing, singing, building, painting, writing or crafting, you love creative self-expression.

12. You have a strong connection with nature and animals

As an empathic and compassionate person, you gravitate towards the natural world. You feel most at home when you're near the ocean or surrounded by trees and animals. Nature is so pure and grounding that you find it a welcome break from the pretension of humanity.

SACRAL CHAKRA

A few inches below your navel

- calming fear
- To heal the inner child

WHAT IS THE INNER CHILD

the term inner child is an individual's childlike aspect. It includes what a person learned as a child, before puberty.

SIGNS OF UNHEALED THE INNER CHILD

An unhealed inner child causes destructive or unhelpful behavior patterns. With a wounded inner child many of us have underlying sense of anxiety or feeling of unease. We wear masks, people please, withdraw, enable, rescue, jump to negative conclusions, act out or become passive aggressive. Or, rather than feeling open, fully alive and free, we feel imprisoned, stuck, stagnant, or weighed down.

- To heal the Intestines

WHAT IS THE INTESTINES

The intestine is a muscular tube which extends from the lower end of your stomach to your anus, the lower opening of the digestive tract. It is also called the bowel or bowels. Food and the products of digestion pass through the intestine, which is divided into two sections called the small intestine and the large intestine.

BENEFITS OF HEALING THE INTESTINES

- For Fatigue
- To improve creativity

WHAT IS CREATIVITY

the use of imagination or original ideas to create something.

BENEFITS OF CREATIVITY

1. BECOME A BETTER PROBLEM SOLVER

There isn't a manual to being an artist, and there isn't a manual for being alive. Obstacles and challenges throughout life are inevitable. However, when we make creativity a habit, we continue to learn new, resourceful ways of solving problems in our artwork, and in life.

2. CONNECT WITH YOUR COMMUNITY

When we create, we connect to other people doing the same

and an instant sense of community is formed. Whether we're exchanging ideas, providing feedback for our peers, or simply creating next to each other in silence, the sense of connection experienced as artists is undeniable and deeply rewarding.

3. SAVE MONEY

Expressing ourselves can control the urge to buy impulsively. If we trade the activity of consuming for creating, we not only save money, but get a deeper sense of fulfillment. Additionally, the more we learn how to make things ourselves, the less we need to spend money on buying them.

4. EXPANDED SENSE OF TIME

Countless artists have discussed the experience of timelessness that one encounters in the creative zone. Time feels limitless when we are in the creative 'zone.' Strangely enough, when we give ourselves time to creative pursuits, we gain time. Who couldn't use the feeling of more time?

5. SELF AWARENESS & EXPRESSION

Creativity is the route to authenticity. As we create, we plumb the depths of our being, accessing what we think and believe. The more we create, the more we discover and realize our habits, impulses, and desires. When we take the time and energy to develop our own ideas, we respect our inner nature and are better able to express ourselves to the world on a regular basis.

6. FREEDOM

There is no right or wrong way to be an artist. When we

create, we are given the opportunity to engage with the world without judging ourselves. We have permission to take risks, try new things, and strip away inhibitions in a healthy way.

7. STRESS RELIEF
Making art is meditative. Taking the time to use our hands, minds, and energy doing something we love is of upmost importance in life. Being creative makes us happy. Art is FUN, and doing anything that brings joy reduces our stress levels and improves our quality of life. What could be more important than that?

- Heals addictions

WHAT ARE ADDICTIONS
Addiction is a psychological and physical inability to stop consuming a chemical, drug, activity, or substance, even though it is causing psychological and physical harm.

- Alcohol addiction
- For cravings

WHAT ARE CRAVINGS
A food cravings is also called selective hunger) is an intense

desire to consume a specific food and is different from normal hunger. can also be a craving for a substance.

- To heal food, binge and comfort eating

WHAT IS COMFORT EATING

Comfort eating is emotional eating is eating as a way to suppress or soothe negative emotions, such as stress, anger, fear, boredom, sadness and loneliness.

- For gambling

WHAT IS GAMBLING

play games of chance for money.

- For sex
- For indigo children

WHAT ARE INDIGO CHILDREN

Indigo children are children who are believed to possess special, unusual, and sometimes supernatural traits or abilities.

DANTIEN CHAKRS

2 fingers below navel

- Centering
- ameliorate aggression

WHAT IS AGGRESSION

the term aggression refers to a range of behaviors that can result in both physical and psychological harm to yourself, others, or objects in the environment. This type of behavior centers on harming another person either physically or mentally.

Aggression can take a variety of forms, including:

- Physical
- Verbal
- Mental
- Emotional

While we often think of aggression as purely in physical forms such as hitting or pushing, psychological aggression can also be very damaging. Intimidating or verbally berating another person, for example, are examples of verbal, mental, and emotional aggression.

- For depleted or disturbed central nervous system

WHAT IS THE NERVOUS SYSTEM

The nervous system is a complex network of nerves and cells that carry messages to and from the brain and spinal cord to various parts of the body. Description

The nervous system is a highly complex part of an animal that coordinates its actions and sensory information by transmitting signals to and from different parts of its body. The nervous system detects environmental changes that impact the body, then works in tandem with the endocrine system to respond to such events.

- For chronic fatigue syndrome

WHAT IS CHRONIC FATIGUE SYNDROME

The main symptom is feeling extremely tired and generally unwell.

Symptoms vary from person to person, and the severity of symptoms can vary from day to day, or even within a day.

Extreme tiredness (fatigue)

The main symptom of Chronic Fatigue Syndrome is extreme physical and mental tiredness (fatigue) that doesn't go away with rest or sleep. This can make it difficult to carry out everyday tasks and activities.

Most people with Chronic Farique Syndrome describe their fatigue as overwhelming and a different type of tiredness from what they've experienced before.

Other symptoms of chronic fatigue syndrome

Other symptoms include:

- sleep problems, such as insomnia
- muscle or joint pain
- headaches
- a sore throat or sore glands that aren't swollen
- problems thinking, remembering or concentrating
- flu like symptoms
- feeling dizzy or sick
- fast or irregular heartbeats

Exercising usually makes the symptoms worse Sometimes the effect is delayed and you'll feel very tired a few hours after you've exercised, or even the next day.

- To improve creativity
- To heal the endocrine system

WHAT IS THE ENDOCRINE SYSTEM

The endocrine system is a series of glands that produce and secrete hormones that the body uses for a wide range of functions. These control many different bodily functions, including:

- Respiration
- Metabolism
- Reproduction
- Sensory perception
- Movement
- Sexual development
- Growth

Hormones are produced by glands and sent into the bloodstream to the various tissues in the body. They send signals to those tissues to tell them what they are supposed to do. When the glands do not produce the right amount of hormones, diseases develop that can affect many aspects of life.

- For fatigue
- To heal the liver

WHAT IS THE LIVER

Your liver is your body's largest solid organ. This organ is vital to the body's metabolic functions and immune system. Without a functioning liver, a person cannot survive.

The liver's position is mostly in the right upper portion of the stomach, just below the diaphragm. A portion of the liver goes into the left upper abdomen as well.

The liver's major functions are in the metabolic processes of the body. These include:

- breaking down or converting substances

- extracting energy
- making toxins less harmful to the body and removing them from the bloodstream

The liver does this by receiving blood with nutrients from the digestive organs via a vein known as the portal vain

The many cells of the liver, known as hepatocytes, accept and filter this blood. They act as little sorting centers, determining:

- which nutrients should be processed
- what should be stored
- what should be eliminated via the stool
- what should go back to the blood

- To heal the lungs

WHAT IS THE LUNG

The lungs absorb oxygen from the air you breathe in and transfer it into your bloodstream so that it can get to every part of your body. As the cells in your body work, they produce a waste gas called carbon dioxide that is released into the bloodstream. Your lungs get rid of this waste gas when you breathe out. The lungs are self-cleaning organs that will begin to heal themselves once their exposure to pollutants stops, for example, when someone quits smoking.

- To heal obsessions

WHAT IS OBSESSIONS

Obsessions are thoughts, images, or ideas that won't go away, are unwanted and cause extreme distress.

- For chronic tiredness
- Heals the endocrine system

WHAT IS THE ENDOCRINE SYSTEM

The endocrine system is the collection of glands that produce hormones that regulate metabolism, growth and development, tissue function, sexual function, reproduction, sleep, and mood, among other things.

- Heals geometric stress
- Heals the liver
- Heals addictions
- For cravings
- For sex

NAVEL CHAKRA

At tummy button

- Alcohol addiction
- For cravings
- To heal food, binge and comfort eating
- For gambling
- For sex

SOLAR PLEXUS CHAKRA

Hand's breadth above the waist

- To heal the digestive tract

WHAT IS THE DIGESTIVE TRACT

Digestion is the complex process of turning the food you eat into nutrients, which the body uses for energy, growth and cell repair needed to survive. The digestion process also involves creating waste to be eliminated.

The digestive tract (or gastrointestinal tract) is a long twisting tube that starts at the mouth and ends at the anus.It is made up of a series of muscles that coordinate the movement of food and other cells that produce enzymes and hormones to aid in the breakdown of food. Along the way are other 'accessory' organs that are needed for digestion: the gallbladder, liver, and the pancreas.

- To heal the stomach

WHAT IS THE STOMACH

The stomach is a organ in the upper part of the abdomen. It is part of the digestive system, which extends from the mouth to the anus.

- For breathlessness

WHAT IS BREATHLESSNESS

Breathlessness refers to the sensation of shortness of breath or difficulty breathing.

- To heal depression

WHAT IS DEPRESSION

Most people feel sad or depressed at times. It's a normal reaction to loss or life's struggles.

But when intense sadness — including feeling helpless, hopeless, and worthless — lasts for many days to weeks and keeps you from living your life, it may be something more than sadness

DEPRESSION SYMPTOMS

Depression can be more than a constant state of sadness or feeling "blue."

Major depression can cause a variety of symptoms. Some affect your mood, and others affect your body. Symptoms may also be ongoing, or come and go.

- **mood, such as** anger, aggressiveness, irritability, anxiousness, restlessness
- **emotional well-being, such as** feeling empty, sad, hopeless
- **behavior, such as** loss of interest, no longer finding pleasure in favorite activities, feeling tired easily, thoughts of suicide, drinking excessively, using drugs, engaging in high-risk activities
- **sexual interest, such as** reduced sexual desire, lack of sexual performance
- **cognitive abilities, such as** inability to concentrate, difficulty completing tasks, delayed responses during conversations
- **sleep patterns, such as** insomnia, restless sleep, excessive sleepiness, not sleeping through the night
- **physical well-being, such as** fatigue, pains, headache, digestive problems

- For detoxification

- To heal obsession
- For panic attacks
- overcome alienation

WHAT IS PANIC ATTACKS

Panic disorder is an anxiety disorder where you regularly have sudden attacks of panic or fear.

Everyone experiences feelings of anxiety and panic at certain times. It's a natural response to stressful or dangerous situations.

But for someone with panic disorder, feelings of anxiety, stress and panic occur regularly and at any time, often for no apparent reason.

SYMPTOMS OF PANIC ATTACKS

Anxiety

Anxiety is a feeling of unease. It can range from mild to severe, and can include feelings of worry and fear. The most severe form of anxiety is panic.

- a racing heartbeat
- feeling faint
- sweating
- nausea
- chest pain
- shortness of breath
- trembling

- hot flushes
- chills
- shaky limbs
- a choking sensation
- dizziness
- numbness or pins and needles
- dry mouth
- a need to go to the toilet
- ringing in your ears
- a feeling of dread or a fear of dying
- a churning stomach
- a tingling in your fingers
- feeling like you're not connected to your body

Most panic attacks last for between 5 and 20 minutes. Some panic attacks have been reported to last up to an hour.

- To release attachments

WHAT ARE ATTACHMENTS

Attachment is a deep and enduring emotional bond that connects one person to another across time and space.

- To heal food, binge and comfort eating
- For gambling

- For asthma

WHAT IS ASTHMA

Asthma is a common lung condition that causes occasional breathing problems.

The main symptoms of asthma include wheezing and shortness of breath.

- Heals trauma

WHAT IS TRAUMA

Trauma is the response to a deeply distressing or disturbing event that overwhelms an individual's ability to cope, causes feelings of helplessness, diminishes their sense of self and their ability to feel the full range of emotions and experiences.

PALM CHAKRA

Palm of your hands

SPLEEN CHAKRA

Below left armpit

- Blood cleanser

HEART SEED CHAKRA

Over the xiphoid, at the tip of breast bone below the heart chakra

HEART CHAKRA

Center of chest

- chronic anxiety
- To heal Angina
- To heal Jealousy
- Despondency
- Emotional shock
- Generosity

WHAT IS JEALOUSY

jealousy refers to the thoughts or feelings of insecurity fear, and concern over a relative lack of possessions or safety.

Jealousy can consist of one or more emotions such as anger, resentment, inadequacy, helplessness or disgust. In its original meaning, *jealousy* is distinct from envy, though the two terms have popularly

- For high blood pressure
- For panic attacks
- Heals the endocrine system

- For panic attacks
- To release attachments
- Alcohol addiction
- Chronic anxiety
- For hopelessness
- calms emotions
- calming fear

WHAT DOES HOPELESS MEAN

having no expectation of good or success

- For mistrust

WHAT DOES MISTRUST MEAN

be suspicious of; have no confidence in.

HIGHER HEART CHAKRA

Over the thymus, between the heart and throat

- To heal the thymus

WHAT IS THE THYMUS

- The thymus gland, located behind your sternum and

between your lungs, is only active until puberty. The thymus gland will not function throughout a full lifetime, but it has a big responsibility when it's active—helping the body protect itself against autoimmunity, which occurs when the immune system turns against itself. Therefore, the thymus plays a vital role in the lymphatic system (your body's defense network) *and* endocrine system.

- Transform psychic attack into

WHAT IS PSYCHIC ATTACK

It means that someone in your life is sending you harmful thoughts and these can lead to vicious headaches, unclear thought patterns, sleepless nights and generally feeling down or unwell. It could be a colleague at work, an ex-girlfriend/boyfriend or wife/husband, an insecure lover or even someone that simply does not like the way you dress or look.

- To stimulate the Metabolism

WHAT IS THE METABOLISM

Metabolism is the process by which your body converts what you eat and drink into energy. During this complex biochemical process, calories in food and beverages are combined with oxygen to release the energy your body needs to function.

- For breathlessness
- To heal the Endocrine system
- To heal the lungs
- For panic attacks
- Protect
- Heals colds
- For stress

WHAT IS STRESS

Stress is your body's way of responding to any kind of demand or threat. When you sense danger—whether it's real or imagined—the body's defenses kick into high gear in a rapid, automatic process known as the "fight-or-flight" reaction or the "stress response."

The stress response is the body's way of protecting you. When working properly, it helps you stay focused, energetic, and alert. In emergency situations, stress can save your life—giving you extra strength to defend yourself,

SYMPTOMS OF STRESS

Cognitive symptoms:

- Memory problems

- Inability to concentrate
- Poor judgment
- Seeing only the negative
- Anxious or racing thoughts
- Constant worrying

Emotional symptoms:

- Depression or general unhappiness
- Anxiety and agitation
- Moodiness, irritability, or anger
- Feeling overwhelmed
- Loneliness and isolation
- Other mental or emotional health problems

Physical symptoms:

- Aches and pains
- Diarrhea or constipation
- Nausea, dizziness
- Chest pain, rapid heart rate
- Loss of sex drive
- Frequent colds or flu

Behavioral symptoms:

- Eating more or less
- Sleeping too much or too little
- Withdrawing from others
- Procrastinating or neglecting responsibilities
- Using alcohol, cigarettes, or drugs to relax

- Nervous habits (e.g. nail biting, pacing)

- Heals the skin or place over site
- Protects aura

WHAT IS THE AURA

The aura is an electromagnetic energy field that surrounds the body. On an energetic level, auras are said to correspond with our chakras and our overall state of consciousness.

every living human has an energy field around them. Other living things, such as trees, flowers, or animals, can also have an energy field.

- For panic attacks
- To boost hormone

WHAT ARE YOUR HORMONES

Hormones are molecules produced by the endocrine system that send messages to various parts of the body. They help regulate your body's processes, like hunger, blood pressure, and sexual desire. While hormones are essential to reproduction, they are fundamental to *all* the systems of your body. Hormones flow through the whole body, but only affect certain cells designed to receive their messages.

- To stimulate metabolism
- For asthma

THROAT CHAKRA
The center of your throat

- To dispel energy
- For breathlessness
- Heals the throat
- Protection against ill wishing

WHAT IS ILL WISHING MEAN
a person who wishes evil or misfortune to another

THIRD EYE/ BROW CHAKRA
Above and between the eyebrows

- Other peoples thoughts invading
- To heal Headaches
- improve memory
- To lighten burdens

WHAT DOES BURDENS MEAN

something difficult or unpleasant that you have to deal with or worry about:

- To heal the pineal gland

WHAT IS THE PINEAL GLAND

Once called the 'third eye,' the pineal gland is a small gland located deep in the center of the brain. Named for its pine cone shape, this gland secretes melatonin, which plays a role in the body's internal clock.

- For relaxation
- Heals the mental body

WHAT IS THE MENTAL BODY

We are not merely our physical bodies. We have an energy body or aura too. Among the other subtle bodies that form a part of us, the mental body is one. While the mental body is able to carry out other functions like feeling as well, it's primary functions are related to the reception, processing and transmitting of information. While thoughts are logically associated with the mental body, it is not only in thoughts that the mental body is functional. Thoughts in themselves are regarded to be more than simply subjective quality. The mental body has stronger associations with knowledge in huge proportions

- To heal the brain
- To disperse confusion
- For migraine
- To heal obsession

WHAT IS OBSESSION

the control of one's thoughts by a continuous, powerful idea or feelings or the ideas or feelings itself.

- For an overactive mind
- Mind detoxification
- Stop other people's thoughts invading
- Heals the mental body

WHAT IS THE MENTAL BODY

We are not just our physical bodies. We have an energy body or aura too. Among the other subtle bodies that form a part of us, the mental body is one.

The mental permanent seed of the mental body serves also as a storage device where all the records of one's past lives are saved. It is understood as a sort of body made up of thoughts.

- Heals the third eye chakra

WHAT IS THE THIRD EYE CHAKRA

The third eye chakra sits between your brows, and it is connected to your spirituality, broadly construed.

- For insomnia from overactive mind
- To boost hormone
- disperse confusion

ALTA MAJOR CHAKRA
Inside the skull

- Heals the mental body
- To heal the brain
- To heal the endocrine system

SOMA CHAKRA
Above the third eye, at the mid hairline

- Heals the mental body
- To heal the brain
- To disperse confusion
- Protection during astral travel
- To release attachments
- Heals the mental body
- overcome alienation

PAST LIFE CHAKRA
Behind the ears, just above the bony ridge

- For migraine

WHAT IS A MIGRAINE

A migraine is a condition that often causes painful headaches.

A migraine is a condition that often causes painful headaches. A migraine can feel like a throbbing headache, It's not entirely clear what causes migraines. They're known to be triggered by periods, stress, tiredness and certain foods or drinks.

You may be able to reduce your migraines by avoiding things that tend to cause them. Eating and sleeping well and regular exercise can also help.

SYMPTOMS OF A MIGRAINE

Other symptoms include feeling sick and sensitivity to light. Other symptoms include disturbed vision, sensitivity to light, sound and smells, feeling sick and vomiting.
feeling sick
being sick
increased sensitivity to light and sound, which is why many people with a migraine want to rest in a quiet, dark room

Some people also occasionally experience other symptoms,

including:
  sweating
  poor concentration,
  feeling very hot or very cold
  tummy (abdominal) pain
  diarrhea

Not everyone with a migraine experiences these additional symptoms and some people may experience them without having a headache.

- For cravings

CAUSAL VORTEX CHAKRA

3-4 inches above and behind the head

- Heals the mental body
- For cravings

CROWN CHAKRA

On top of head

- Memory improve

METHODS TO IMPROVE YOUR MEMORY

Focus Your Attention

Attention is one of the major components of memory. In order for information to move from your short-term memory into your long-term memory, you need to attend to this information. Try to study in a place free of distractions such as television, music, and other diversions.

Avoid Cramming

Studying materials over a number of sessions gives you the time you need to process information.

Read Out Loud

reading materials out loud significantly improves your memory of the material.

Get Some Sleep

sleep is important for memory and learning.

- To lighten burdens
- For wisdom

WHAT IS WISDOM

Wisdom is the quality of having experience, knowledge, and good judgment; the quality of being wise.

Wisdom is the ability to think and act using knowledge,

experience, understanding, common sense and insight.

- To heal the crown chakra
- To heal the brain
- Improves memory
- For migraine
- Balances and aligns the crown chakra
- Crown chakra spin too rapid and chakra stuck open

WHAT IS THE CROWN CHAKRA

The crown chakra is a swirling energy center on top of your head.

The crown chakra is our connector to the divine and our spiritual nature. It also allows for spirituality to integrate into our physical lives. the Crown Chakra is the entry point for the human life-force which pours abundantly into the body's energy system from the greater universe, It is this force that nourishes the body, mind, and spirit, and it distributes this energy throughout the physical body and down the lower chakras. The seventh chakra which is the crown chakra influences the major body systems: the eleven organ systems, which are made of multiple organs that work together to keep the human body functioning

The main systems of the human body are:

1. circulatory systems

- Circulates blood around the body via the heart arteries

and veins, delivering oxygen and nutrients to organs and cells and carrying their waste products away.
- Keeps the body's temperature in a safe range.

1. Digestive system and Excretory system

- System to absorb nutrients and remove waste via the gastrointestinal tract including the mouth, esophagus, stomach and intestines
- Eliminates waste from the body.

1. Endocrine system

- Influences the function of the body using hormones.

1. Integurmentary system / Exocrine system

- skin, hair, nails,sweat and other exocrine system

1. immune systems and lymphatic system

- Defends the body against pathogens that may harm the body.
- The system comprising a network of lymphatic vessels that carry a clear fluid called lymph.
- Muscular system
- Enables the body to move using muscles.

1. Nervous system

- Collects and processes information from the senses via

nerves and the brain and tells the muscles to contract to cause physical actions.

1. Renal system and urinary system

- The system where the kidneys filter blood to produce urine and get rid of waste.

1. Reproductive system

- The reproductive system required for the production of offspring.

1. Respiratory system

- Brings air into and out of the lungs to absorb oxygen and remove carbon dioxide

1. Skeletal system

- Bones maintain the structure of the body and its organs.

On an emotional level, the Crown Chakra generates devotion, inspirational and prophetic thought, mystical connections and transcendental ideas.

HIGHER CROWN CHAKRA

Just above the crown chakra, above the head

SOUL STAR CHAKRA
6 inches above head

- For indigo children

STELLAR GATEWAY
12 inches above head

- For indigo children

EFFECTIVE HEALING TIP THAT WORKS

Please heal every single chakra with a amethyst as if you take a look at the Amethyst healing properties in this book the Amethyst will heal those issues in each and every chakra and there is more what an Amethyst heals then what is known.

What I do before I go to bed for the night I tape the Amethyst to each and every chakra with some strong diy household or parcel tape except the ones on my back and for my head and soma and past life and throat chakras I cut up a pair of tights long enough to tie around my head like a head band and place the Amethyst in the head band on my chakras I do the same for my throat chakra, then in the day time everyday in my spare time I lay on the floor for 20 minutes to one hour with the

Amethyst on the chakras above my head and below my feet and on my back chakras and lay on my front and I use a clothes measuring tape for exact location of them chakras below my feet and above my head and subtle bodies and I heal with the amethyst on every chakra every day and night for 6 weeks, you are guaranteed to be healed and issues to be healed, after such an healing session and you will feel so much better. Most people just heal one chakra then say it does not work I am not healed but they have healed just one chakra and just for an hour, the issues are in all those other chakras what you have and you need to heal more than once as there could be really deep issues or ill health so I hope you take on board my tip for healing as it works I do this with each different crystal I work with so I heal for six weeks then I have a rest for a week or two weeks then get an other crystal and heal for six weeks and so on.

III

Part Three

Seventeen

Recommended Authors

I recommend Judy Hall books to read, Judy Hall is amazing Author with so much information about crystals and subtle bodies ect, her books are easy to read and to understand and has really interesting content, you can learn so much from Judy Hall, i also recommend Judy Halls website where you can buy healing crystals and subscribe to a payed subscription to join a crystal community group where you can get help and advice about healing crystals.

Printed in Great Britain
by Amazon

83486938R00106